THE
KOREAN
WAR

DEAN ACHESON

THE
KOREAN
WAR

W · W · NORTON & COMPANY · INC · NEW YORK

Library of Congress Catalog Card No. 72-141578

SBN 393 09978 4

1 2 3 4 5 6 7 8 9 0

CONTENTS

INTRODUCTION   1

Events Leading Up to the Attack. The Underlying
Causes of the Korean Conflict. Sinister Purposes and
Mistaken Beliefs. Soviet Aggressive Moves Begin.
The Blockade of Berlin. A Year of Growing Tension.

I. THE ATTACK   15

Saturday, June 24. Sunday, June 25. Monday, June 26.
Tuesday, June 27. Wednesday, June 28. Thursday,
June 29. Friday, June 30.

II. THE FIRST CRISIS   32

An Anxious Summer. Anglo-Indian Peace Initiatives.
Arms and the Men. MacArthur Drops Some Bricks.
From Retreat to Counteroffensive. Conflict over a
Boundary. Uniting for Peace. Long-range Policy and
Crossing the Parallel. Instructions to General Mac-
Arthur. "A Unified, Independent and Democratic Korea."

III. LOST CHANCES   60

Pilgrimage to Wake. MacArthur Moves North.
Schizophrenia at GHQ. The Last Clear Chance.

IV. "AN ENTIRELY NEW WAR"   73

Disaster Rattles the General. Washington Plans
Next Moves. Steady As You Go. The Attlee Visit.

V.   ATTEMPTS TO STABILIZE THE WAR   92
       On the Korean Front. On the United Nations
       Front. On the Tokyo Front. The Parallel Once More.
       The Final Showdown.

VI.   THE RELIEF OF GENERAL MAC ARTHUR   104
       The Days of Decision. The Communications Mix-up.
       The Senate Hearings. Reflections.

VII.   THE MOVE FOR AN ARMISTICE   115
       Peace Feelers. The Kennan-Malik Talks. The Decision
       to Negotiate Through Ridgway. Foul-up as Negotiations
       Start. Negotiations Off and Fighting On. Negotiations
       Resumed at Panmunjom.

VIII.   CRISIS OVER PRISONERS OF WAR   128
       Voluntary Repatriation of Prisoners. Revolt in the
       Compounds. Bombing Bothers Britain.

IX.   AN OPEN COVENANT OPENLY CONNIVED   137
       AGAINST
       The Central Issue and Its Ambiance. The Menon
       Cabal. A Showdown Impends. Canadian Interlude
       and Finale.

AFTERWORD   149

INDEX   151

MAPS

NORTH KOREAN PEOPLE'S ARMY INVASION   17

LANDING AT INCHON   48

CHINESE–NORTH KOREAN INTERVENTION ATTACK   75

CHINESE–NORTH KOREAN OFFENSIVE AND U.N. COUNTERATTACK   117

INTRODUCTION

Events Leading Up to the Attack

OCCUPATION OF KOREA—American or otherwise—was never more than a temporary expedient of the United States Government, and then only as a means of liquidating the Japanese rule over that country. Prior to annexation by Japan in 1910, control of Korea had been the subject of intense rivalry between China and Russia. During World War II the allied powers had agreed on a free and independent Korea with a preliminary, and hopefully brief, trusteeship. Japan's sudden collapse precipitated arrangements for the surrender of her considerable forces in Korea. The Joint Chiefs of Staff proposed that the United States accept surrender in the south, nearest Japan; and the Russians in the north, nearest Siberia. A young officer recently returned to the Pentagon from the China-India-Burma theater, Colonel Dean Rusk, found a convenient administrative dividing line along the 38th parallel. This would give the United States a northern port of embarkation at Inchon and a southern one at Pusan to facilitate repatriation of the surrendered troops. The plan, accepted by President Truman on August 14, 1945, and by Marshal Stalin, on August 16, was promulgated by General Douglas MacArthur in General Order No. 1 on September 2, 1945. But almost at once, as General John R. Hodge, in command in Korea, reported, "dissatisfaction with the division of the country" began. He soon found that the Soviet Union considered the 38th parallel not a line of military administrative convenience but a wall delimiting their preserve. Commanders were having the same experience with Soviet forces in Germany, Berlin, and Iran. They were resisting a similar effort in Austria and the effort of the

Soviet Government to place its troops in American-occupied Japan.

Secretary of State James F. Byrnes and Soviet Foreign Minister Vyacheslav Molotov took up the problem in Moscow in December 1945, working out an agreement for a joint commission to bring about the unity and independence of Korea. For nearly two years Soviet members frustrated every effort made through the commission. Finally Secretary of War Robert Patterson recommended that we withdraw our troops from Korea to meet greater needs for our shrinking military resources elsewhere. The President having approved, the United States on September 17, 1947, laid the question of Korean independence and the withdrawal of foreign troops before the United Nations General Assembly and submitted a resolution on October 28 calling for withdrawal of troops after elections of local representatives of North and South to work out unification. Interpreting this as what it was, an attempt to terminate our responsibilities in Korea, the Russians accepted withdrawal and opposed United Nations-supervised elections. They proposed leaving it to North and South Koreans to agree on unification without interference after foreign withdrawal. This plain invitation to civil war was rejected and a revised and amended American resolution was adopted. On May 10, 1948, the UN election commission, barred from the North, held elections in the South, and Syngman Rhee was elected President of the Republic of Korea. On August 15, 1948, American military government ended. The Russians responded by creating a People's Republic of Korea in the North, which also claimed jurisdiction over the entire country. The Republic of Korea was recognized as the lawful government by the General Assembly on December 12, and by the United States on January 1, 1949.

On September 19, 1948, the Soviet Foreign Office in Moscow had informed our Embassy that their troops would be withdrawn by the end of December. We had our troops out by the end of June 1949, leaving only a small training mission.

Economic aid by civilian staff, however, continued. For the fiscal year 1950 (ending June 30) Congress had appropriated sixty million dollars for economic aid to be spent before February 15, 1950. On June 7, 1949, the President asked for an additional one hundred fifty million dollars for the rest of the fiscal year. "The Korean problem," we said, "is one upon which we must act. . . . If we do not do it, we are absolutely certain that the whole situation in Korea will collapse and Korea will fall into the Communist area." [1] However, the House and Senate reached unreconcilable

1. House Committee on Foreign Affairs, 81st Cong., 1st Sess., *Hearings on HR 5330, Korean Aid*, pp. 191–92.

positions.

On January 19, 1950, came a bitter and unexpected blow. "This has been a tough day," I wrote to my daughter, "not so much by way of work, but by way of troubles. We took a defeat in the House on Korea, which seems to me to have been our own fault. One should not lose by one vote. [The vote was 193 to 192.] We were complaisant and inactive. We have now a long road back."

The vehicle of this trouble was not an important or controversial bill, but a comparatively small supplemental appropriation for aid to Korea. It seemed so small and harmless that we neglected our usual precautions and were caught off guard by a combination of China-bloc Republicans and economy-minded southern Democrats and defeated on a snap vote.

The President expressed our "concern and dismay" over what had occurred and called for its early remedy. An extension of the China Aid Act for a few months was joined with the Korean appropriation and a little sweetening added for congressional adherents of Chiang Kai-shek. The new bill became law on February 14, 1950. But damage had been done. Without question, the government and people of the United States wished to end their responsibility for the government and future of Korea. Apparently, however, the impression was given that both would tolerate having this responsibility ended by force from the outside, even though this force should be created, organized, and launched by the Soviet Union as part of a series of moves against the position and purposes of the United States.[2]

The Underlying Causes of the Korean Conflict

Korea furnished more the locus than the cause of a trial by battle with the Soviet Union. Since the defeat and surrender of Germany and Japan, the disappearance of the great empires of Europe, and the eclipse of China, the United States and the Soviet Union had emerged unrivaled—save each by the other—among the powers of earth. Each had been molded by its position, its experience, and its conception of its interests to view the other with distrust amounting to hostility. Unfortunately, but inevitably, this attitude has affected the replacement of the old world-order of the nineteenth century, European-oriented and based upon the dominance and concert of the great European empires. Even now, after a

2. At the time, it was asserted by partisan opponents of the Administration that a speech made by the author at the National Press Club on January 12, 1950, had given support to this impression. This argument is fully discussed in Dean Acheson, *Present at the Creation* (New York: W. W. Norton & Company, 1969), pp. 355–58.

quarter of a century, agreement has been impossible. Only an uneasy *modus vivendi*, based upon a balance of terror between the superpowers, has led them to place some restraint upon their client-states among the emerging states. That too is wearing very thin in Southeast Asia and the eastern Mediterranean. In North Korea the omens were read to call not for restraint but its opposite; and war resulted.

Years ago Elihu Root observed:

When foreign affairs were ruled by autocracies or oligarchies the danger of war was in sinister purpose. When foreign affairs are ruled by democracies the danger of war will be in mistaken beliefs.

Mr. Root assumed that the danger of war came and would come from the conflict of nations ruled by the same type of government. But today that is not so. Would his formula lead us to conclude, however, that the danger of war between the Soviet oligarchy and the American democracy lies in both sinister purpose and mistaken beliefs? There is a good deal of evidence to support that view.

Sinister Purposes and Mistaken Beliefs

American Attitudes · The nature of the world around us is one thing; American notions about it are quite another. Two contrary and equally unrealistic ideas about it compete for the national mind, both springing from our earlier history. From the American phases of the European wars of the eighteenth century—the dominant memory of the founders of this country—came the doctrine promulgated in President Washington's farewell address, called isolationism. From the experience of the long period of world peace and economic development in the nineteenth century following the settlement of Vienna in 1815 and the British Navy's support of the Monroe Doctrine, came the dream of universal law and internationally enforced peace, embodied and embalmed in the League of Nations and resurrected in the United Nations. Both involve mistaken beliefs.

The wars of the eighteenth century sprang from causes deeper than dynastic rivalries. For a century and a quarter French power—whether directed by the Bourbon monarchy, the French republic, or the Bonapartist empire—drove with immense vitality for hegemony in Europe, North America, the West Indies, the Middle East, and South Asia. It was present and aggressive in North America, determined to keep the English settlements pinned between the

Atlantic and the eastern slopes of the Alleghenies. The long struggle ended only at Waterloo.

Military defeat and the statesmanship of Metternich, Castlereagh, and Talleyrand brought about a settlement of the wars with France. It permitted a century of international peace and of greater technological and economic development than had occurred in the whole period since the invention of the sail and wheel. But it was George Canning who, by putting the sanction of the British fleet behind the Monroe Doctrine, made sure that the scattered and divided nine million Americans, with their center of population a few miles west of their capital city, could attack the enormous task of occupying an unexplored continent free from interference from Europe's hundred and ninety million, or any part of them.

Thus, in the Europe-oriented-and-dominated world of the nineteenth century, the Western Hemisphere became out of bounds for colonial expansion. But not for investment. Europe, after a few years of doubt, stood ready to invest in the American gamble. Throughout the century the flood of "foreign aid" grew and grew, until in the half-century preceding 1914, Western Europe, led by Great Britain, "had invested abroad almost as much as the entire national wealth of Great Britain. . . . If the same proportion of American resources were devoted to foreign investment as Britain devoted . . . in 1913, the flow of investment would require to be thirty times as great. The entire Marshall Plan would have to be carried out twice a year." [3]

Economically the globe was indeed "one world." The great empires of Europe, through their colonies and spheres of influence, spread authority, order, and respect for the obligation of contract almost everywhere; and where their writs did not run, their frigates and gunboats navigated. Methods were rough, division of benefits was unfair, and freedom was not rated high among the priorities; but people, goods, and ideas moved around the world with less restraint than ever before and, perhaps, ever again. The outlook of many Europeans was reflected by Tennyson's "Locksley Hall" (1842):

> Till the war drum throbbed no longer,
>   and the battle flags were furled
> In the Parliament of Man, the Federation
>   of the World.

3. A. K. Cairncross, *Home and Foreign Investment, 1870–1913* (Cambridge: Cambridge University Press, 1953), p. 3.

> There the common sense of most shall hold
> a fretful realm in awe,
> And the kindly earth shall slumber,
> lapt in universal law.[4]

Russian Attitudes · Even before V-E day, Stalin had already vindicated Churchill's view of the Soviet intention to make Eastern Europe a Russian satellite area.

On February 9, 1946, before a vast "election" audience in Moscow, Stalin stated with brutal clarity the Soviet Union's postwar policy.[5] Finding the causes of the late war in the necessities of capitalist-imperialist monopoly and the same forces still in control abroad, he concluded that no peaceful international order was possible. The Soviet Union must, therefore, be capable of guarding against any eventuality. The basic materials of national defense—iron and steel—must be trebled, and coal and oil, the sources of energy, doubled. Consumer goods, so desperately needed in Russia, must wait on rearmament. This grim news depressed even the ebullient spirits of Secretary of State Byrnes. They were soon to be depressed even further.

In response to a request for elucidation of this startling speech, George F. Kennan, then Chargé d'Affaires in Moscow, cabled a long and truly remarkable dispatch. It had a deep effect on thinking within the Government, although Government response with action still needed a year's proof of Soviet intentions as seen by Kennan. He found "at the bottom of the Kremlin's neurotic view of world affairs" centuries of a Russian fear of physical, and a tyranny's fear of political, insecurity. To the Government, whether czarist or bolshevik, penetration by the Western world was its greatest danger.

---

4. The contemporary American attitude of missionary evangelicism in foreign policy was emotionally stated in President Lyndon B. Johnson's Inaugural Address on January 20, 1965:

> Our destiny in the midst of change will rest on the unchanged character of our people and on their faith. They came here—the exile and the stranger, brave but frightened—to find a place where a man could be his own man. They made a covenant with this land. Conceived in justice, written in liberty, bound in union, it was meant one day to inspire the hopes of all mankind, and it binds us still. If we keep its terms, we shall flourish. . . .
>
> The American covenant called on us to help show the way for the liberation of man, and that is our goal. Thus, if as a nation, there is much outside our control, as a people no stranger is outside our hope.
>
> . . . Terrific dangers and troubles that we once called "foreign" now constantly live among us. If American lives must end, and American treasure be spilled, in countries that we barely know, then that is the price that change has demanded of conviction and of our enduring covenant. . . .
>
> For we are a nation of believers . . . in justice and liberty and union. . . . We believe that every man must some day be free.

111 *Congressional Record*, 89th Congress, 1st Session, pp. 985–86.
5. For text, see *The New York Times*, February 10, 1946.

Marxism "with its basic altruism of purpose" furnished them with justification for their "fear of [the] outside world. . . . In the name of Marxism they sacrificed every single ethical value in their methods and tactics. Today they cannot dispense with it. It is [the] fig leaf of their moral and intellectual respectability."

Kennan predicted that Soviet policy would be to use every means to infiltrate, divide, and weaken the West. Means would include the foreign communist parties, diplomacy, international organizations—blocking what they did not like, starting false trails to divert—probing weak spots by every means. To seek a *modus vivendi* with Moscow would prove chimerical, a process leading not to an end but only to political warfare. His recommendations—to be of good heart, to look to our own social and economic health, to present a good face to the world, all of which the Government was trying to do—were of no help; his historical analysis might or might not have been sound, but his predictions and warnings could not have been better.[6] We responded to them slowly.

Although Kennan sounded the alarm from Moscow, more than a year went by before the Kremlin's actions drove home to Americans in Congress, the executive branch, the press, and (increasingly) the public that their late ally regarded them now as its principal enemy. The Russians' history had taught them for centuries, as Kennan stated, that "penetration by the Western world was [their] greatest danger." Slavonic forest tribes had lived since early in the Christian era on the southern Eurasian plain between the Dnieper and the Dniester rivers without natural defenses. Conquerors had swept over them from the east and from the west. From the twelfth century on, a Slavonic nucleus emerged as areas called grand duchies fought themselves free from alien rule, amalgamated, and grew by overland expansion—not as the British had, after consolidating their island base, by overseas conquest. Existence itself had always been based on immense military power.

Thus, in dealing with the outside world, the Soviet Union followed its Russian past in seeking to expand outward along its borders, since strong neighbors were bound to be enemies and dangerous, while weak ones were natural victims. From its imperial past came, also, belief in the necessity of military power superior to any that might threaten. The destruction of German and Japanese armaments had only led to American emergence on the world scene in possession of nuclear weapons. No American protestations of a desire for international control of this doomsday weapon removed

6. George F. Kennan, *Memoirs: 1925–1950* (Boston: Little, Brown and Company, 1967), pp. 547–59.

from us the stigma of being the Soviets' principal enemy and threat.

From its Marxian present the Soviet Union drew a fanatical and fighting faith which taught the inevitability of victory over the hostile capitalist world. Just such a faith swept Islam almost to dominance of Eurasia between the seventh and fifteenth centuries.

Soviet Aggressive Moves Begin

Upon German surrender in 1945, the Soviet Union occupied and placed under military rule territories on its western and southwestern borders from the Baltic to northern Iran. In 1946 probes began into contiguous territories to test the possibility of further penetration. Turkey was pressed to agree to joint Soviet-Turkish defense of the straits and the entrance to the Black Sea. Soviet troops refused to evacuate the oil fields of northern Iran, which had been occupied during the war to anticipate German seizure. Both moves were met by determined resistance by the countries involved, with sturdy support from the United States and such political backing as the infant United Nations could lend.

As fast as Soviet probes were blocked, new ones were made. Sensing increasing weakness in what had been areas of British responsibility for support, Communist guerrilla pressure on eastern Turkey (Kars-Ardahan) and northern Greece was increased. Bands retreated, when pressed, across the Yugoslav border. In February 1947, the British could go on no longer and informed us that after another month their aid to Greece and Turkey through funds, supplies, and troops would have to stop. After an urgent analysis of the needs, dangers, and possibilities, President Truman asked a joint session of Congress, in a message that came to be known as the Truman Doctrine, for authority and funds for assistance to Greece and Turkey. The authority was to detail civilians and military personnel to Greece and Turkey upon request to supervise the use of the aid furnished and to train Greeks and Turks. The House and Senate granted the President's request by large and bipartisan majorities.

Our aid to Greece and Turkey, which continued for several years, was vastly supplemented by a major error of the Soviet Union and intervention by nature. In June 1948, growing interference by Moscow in Yugoslav affairs and resistance to it in Belgrade led to a break between the two Communist dictatorships, expulsion of Yugoslavia from the Cominform and the Communist alliances, interruption of economic relations with Yugoslavia by other Communist states, and intensive Soviet propaganda attacks. The United

States discreetly supplied economic help to Yugoslavia, which increased when, shortly, a severe drought struck that country's agriculture. Guerrilla raids conducted from Yugoslavia across the border into the south, most helpfully, stopped.

Soviet obstruction turned elsewhere. In 1946, the United States made proposals for the international control of atomic energy and weapons. The Soviet Union threw itself into violent opposition so that the proposal came to nothing. The proposal for a commission for the international control of atomic energy posed especially difficult problems for the Soviet Union. Its violent opposition, which led to the defeat of the proposals, can in part be attributed to what has already been said here about the history of Russia's attitude toward reliance upon her own armament and to her distrust of international guarantees. Here was a case where a sinister purpose grew at least partially out of mistaken beliefs. The Soviet Government was determined that no sort of limitation or control of nuclear energy should be agreed upon until Soviet armament equal to any had been achieved. Bernard M. Baruch, whom President Truman had appointed as U.S. Representative on the United Nations Atomic Energy Commission, put forward for the United States proposals containing provision for "condign punishment" for a violator of the proposed self-denying treaty. This could be and was interpreted as preparation for an anti-Soviet alliance should the Soviet Union break away from a plan with which that government disagreed. Probably any other approach would have failed, as subsequent experience indicates, to gain Soviet approval of international control to the extent sought in 1946. All of Soviet history would have set the Russians against any system that would have seemed to have made possible, realistically, Soviet inferiority to the United States in nuclear weapons.

Not long after this blow had dimmed war-born hopes of peace through universal law internationally agreed, administered, and enforced, new and major difficulties arose with the Soviet Union at what seemed to be the most crucial point of contact between East and West—Europe and the four-power administration of Germany. The difficulties grew out of the collapse of another illusion.

American ideas about the treatment of defeated Germany had changed greatly since the harsh occupation policy laid down in April 1945, by Joint Chiefs of Staff directive (JCS 1067) for the military government of the American zone. This was an uneasy blending of State, War, and Treasury Department ideas. It was punitive, repressive, aimed at exacting reparations, preventing German rearmament, Nazism, and better conditions of life in Germany than among the victims of German aggression. Almost at once, however, the policy was seen by those executing it to be unworkable. Conditions in Europe and Germany's relation to them had been misjudged. The danger was deterioration so fast and so far as to carry all Western Europe to total social, economic, and political disintegration. Such a Europe would fall an easy prey to Communist propaganda.

The Soviet Union had already divided Europe; it now seized the opportunity to keep Germany divided into small zones, preventing any recovery of economic strength, German self-respect, or the opportunity to play a useful role in a European community. At every turn, both in the quadripartite control of Germany and in the effort to bring about a common European approach to reconstruction, the Soviet Union obstructed. Again, nature intervened most drastically in high policy.

Europe emerged from German military rule to face the tasks of re-establishing governments, order, and internal confidence; repairing war damage; restoring (without the capital or materials) a peacetime industry. Soon another problem emerged—re-activating agriculture after two winters of a severity unequaled in current memory. All planning proved totally inadequate. The whole organized means of sustaining life in Europe was close to total paralysis.

At this moment, on June 5, 1947, the United States Government proposed the Marshall Plan. Before the United States could help Europe start on its way to recovery,

there must be some agreement among the countries of Europe as to the requirements of the situation and the part those countries themselves will take in order to give proper effect to whatever action might be undertaken by this Government.
. . . .
The program should be a joint one, agreed to by a number, if not all, European nations.

The role of this country should consist of friendly aid in the drafting of a European program and of later support of such a program so far as it may be practical for us to do so.[7]

A meeting of European nations convened at once in Paris. After a few days the Soviet Union denounced the Marshall Plan and withdrew from the meeting; thereafter no Communist government would have any connection with it. The other European states went forward with this joint recovery program in which the

7. *Department of State Bulletin*, Vol. XVI, June 15, 1947, p. 1160.

United States put $9.7 billion to achieve the brilliant restoration of Europe.

The Soviet Union, having failed to prevent the inception of the program, undertook to sabotage it. The attack centered upon preventing Germany's playing its necessary role in European life. Events moved swiftly to crisis. By Communist coup in February 1948, in which Jan Masaryk, foreign minister and son of the founder of the Czechoslovak republic, met his death, that nation was added to the Soviet satellites. On March 17 the Western European Allies signed the Brussels Defense Pact. Three days later the Soviet representative walked out of the Allied Control Council in Berlin, and on April 1 Soviet authorities imposed restrictions on allied (but not German) rail and road traffic between the western zones and Berlin. The allies responded with the "little airlift" to supply, at this time, only their troops in Berlin.

In the meantime a six-nation negotiating group—the three occupying West Germany and the three Benelux governments—went to work on plans to strengthen Germany against developing Russian pressure. Preliminary recommendations in late March, as the Foreign Assistance Act for 1948 became law, provided for economic coordination of the three zones for association in the European Recovery Program, and broad agreement that a federal form of government was best adapted to eventual German unity. Final recommendations, announced in June from London, covered political institutions for the West Germans with "the minimum requirements of occupation and control." To reassure the French, provision was made for the control of the Ruhr and the continuance of supreme allied authority.

The Blockade of Berlin

These recommendations and the much-needed currency reform for West Germany (though, at this time, not for Berlin, still regarded as under four-power control) triggered the final break with the Soviet Union in Germany. The calendar for June 1948 shows its precipitous course.

June 7 London recommendations announced.

June 11 Soviet Union stops rail traffic between Berlin and West for two days.

June 12 Soviets stop traffic on a highway bridge for "repairs."

June 16 Soviet representative leaves Kommandatura (four-power military control in Berlin).

June 18 Western powers announce currency reform in West Germany.
June 23 Soviet Union orders its own currency system for East Germany and all Berlin.
         Western powers extend West German currency reform to West Berlin.
June 24 Soviet Union imposes full blockade on Berlin.
         Western powers stop freight from combined zones to Soviet zone.

After a difficult and tense period in which the calm determination of General Lucius D. Clay, the Deputy for military government of the American Zone, steadied our own government and held our allies together, the Western powers settled down to build up the airlift, tighten their own countermeasures against the Soviet Union, and fight the propaganda battle in the Paris sessions of the United Nations, which proved unable to ameliorate the situation. Soviet authorities, meanwhile, though belligerent in words, were careful to avoid physical interference with the airlift. The combined lift increased from seventy thousand tons in June and July 1948 to two hundred fifty thousand tons in May 1949.

By the spring of 1949 the airlift was a demonstrated success and the allied counter-measures against communication with East Germany were imposing severe pressure there. Stalin decided that the blockade had been a failure and opened secret negotiations with Washington to call it off. The Western allies, now thoroughly aware of the necessity of strength in dealing with Moscow, had been active. Negotiation of the North Atlantic Treaty was hurried to completion, and it was signed on April 4, 1949.[8] However, neither the United States nor any of its allies was prepared to furnish the military aid that the treaty contemplated in case of attack on any of them.

On May 4, 1949, agreement was reached with the Russians to end the blockade and counter-blockade on May 12 and to consider, at a Foreign Ministers' meeting convened in Paris on May 23, problems arising out of Berlin. This ended the Berlin crisis, but the conference accomplished nothing except to demonstrate the irreconcilable gap between the Soviet Union and the Western allies. The Soviet purpose to prevent any movement toward unification and creation of German government, and the allied purpose to

---

8. 63 *U.S. Statutes*, Part 2, pp. 2242–53. The countries signing were Belgium, Canada, Denmark, France, Iceland, Italy, Luxembourg, the Netherlands, Norway, Portugal, United Kingdom, United States. On February 18, 1952, Greece and Turkey deposited instruments of accession to the North Atlantic Treaty.

clarify and strengthen rights of access to Berlin both failed completely after a month of useless talk.

A Year of Growing Tension

In the year between the adjournment of the Foreign Ministers' Conference in Paris (June 20, 1949) and the attack on South Korea (June 25, 1950), tension between the two great powers mounted at every point. Four main developments marked its growth.

In September 1949, the Soviet Union exploded its first nuclear device. This was considerably in advance of our own experts' prediction and stimulated our own review of our military position, both nuclear and conventional. We were still planning on a defense budget for the fiscal year ending June 30, 1950, of fourteen and a half billion dollars, which contemplated continued demobilization of our wartime military establishment. Soldiers, scientists, and the public were still debating the possibility of developing a still more powerful nuclear weapon, the hydrogen bomb, new vehicles for delivering it, and the wisdom and morality of attempting to do so. It was now plain that the Soviet decision in favor of nuclear competition rather than cooperation in reduction and control was bearing fruit rapidly. At the year's end a committee of the Secretaries of State and Defense, with the Chairman of the Atomic Energy Commission, advised the President, who agreed, to proceed with the effort to develop a hydrogen weapon.

At the same time another committee of the National Security Council was reviewing our foreign and military policies in view of the rapidly changing world situation. In April 1950, it advised the President in a paper known as NSC-68 that the immediate outlook called for an end to demobilization and for increased military force, both nuclear and conventional, and a tightening of our alliances to meet increased threats from many quarters. The President approved.

In Europe, the blockade of Berlin had induced a new chill of fear of Russian intentions and ruthlessness, together with accompanying hope that salvation might be found in a bold and strong allied counteraction, such as had defeated the blockade. This meant a change of attitude and purpose within the Western alliance from that of liberation after attack, as in the late war, to prevention of attack. The latter would require a large military assistance program from the United States to arm our European allies, and considerable American and European forces in existence and in place, under a unified command. Looming in the background was the problem of Germany. The Germans were feared and distrusted by Europeans, allies and Russians alike. A European defense seemed impossible without the Germans, and trouble seemed highly likely if they were included. In either event, tension with the Communist bloc would be increased.

In the United States the reaction to the final defeat of Chiang Kai-shek in China and his withdrawal to Formosa (Taiwan) in December 1949, raised intense political controversy. Right-wing opponents of the Administration charged it with "the loss of China," with being "soft on communism," and the isolationists charged it with endless commitment of American dollars and soldiers to Europe. Here were troubled waters aplenty in which Soviet propaganda could cause trouble.

In such a setting as this we were looking forward to a weekend of comparative rest on Saturday, June 24, 1950.

I

THE ATTACK

MIDSUMMER'S DAY, 1950, passed without any pricking of our thumbs to warn us of grave trouble to come just beyond this turning of the year. On Saturday, June 24, my wife and I escaped Washington for a quiet weekend at Harewood Farm. As quiet, that is, as that haven could then be. The white telephone tied into the White House switchboard was used sparingly by considerate associates, but it was used. Even when evening came and the busy world was hushed and the fever of day was over, the movements of the security officers changing guard during the night echoed through that small house. The crank mail, which Wisconsin Senator Joseph Mc-Carthy's attentions had increased, led to the undesired innovation of night as well as day shifts of guards around me, a regimen not conducive to relaxation. However, the weekend began well. After some hours of gardening and a good dinner I had turned in to read myself to sleep.

Saturday, June 24

About ten o'clock the White House telephone had me up again. John Hickerson, Assistant Secretary for United Nations Affairs, Dean Rusk, Assistant Secretary for Far Eastern Affairs, and Philip C. Jessup, Ambassador at Large, had been called to the Department by a cable from our Ambassador in Seoul, Korea, John Muccio, an experienced and level-headed officer, reporting an attack from the north across the 38th parallel on South Korean forces. It described a heavy attack, different from patrol forays that had occurred in the past, and in Muccio's opinion was an all-out offensive against the Republic of Korea.

This cable had crossed an inquiry from the Department stimulated by disturbing press rumors out of Seoul. Hickerson and the others were in touch with Frank Pace, Secretary of the Army; Louis Johnson, Secretary of Defense, and General Omar N. Bradley, Chairman of the Joint Chiefs of Staff, were in Tokyo. Other Chiefs of Staff had not yet been located, and former Senator Warren Austin, our Ambassador at the United Nations, was at his home in Burlington, Vermont. Asked for a recommendation, Hickerson suggested a meeting of the UN Security Council the next morning (Sunday) to call for a cease-fire, and urgent requests to our civilian and military missions in Korea for continuing information.

I approved, and authorized Ernest Gross, Ambassador Austin's deputy, to ask Secretary General Trygve Lie to call the Security Council. Overnight Hickerson, Rusk, and Jessup were to work with the Pentagon through Frank Pace to get up such orders as the President might wish to issue should he decide to take further action, military or otherwise. Meanwhile I would telephone the President, who was spending the weekend at his home in Independence, Missouri. Any changes he wished to make in my instructions could easily overtake them.

Clock time in Independence, calculated on Central Standard Time, read two hours earlier than ours in Washington. The President had just finished a family dinner when he came to the telephone and learned the situation and the instructions given. He approved and suggested his immediate return to Washington. I dissuaded him from adding the unnecessary risk of a hurriedly arranged night flight and urged instead a further report from me next morning, when our information should be more complete, and his return to Washington later in the day. He agreed and asked whether he could do anything to help us overnight. Remembering that Louis Johnson had imposed rigid restrictions on communication between the two departments, I asked the President to let Frank Pace know that he wanted the fullest cooperation between the departments. No difficulty of any sort developed in work between them. A call of confirmation to Hickerson completed my night's work, but not his.

Sunday, June 25

The next morning at the Department the news was bad. A full-scale attack centering around a tank column was driving toward Seoul and Kimpo airport. South Korean arms were clearly outclassed. Recommendations had been prepared by the two departments for

NORTH KOREAN PEOPLES ARMY
INVASION AND EXPLOITATION
25 June – 15 Sept. 1950

Vladivostok

U.S.S.R.

MANCHURIA

HUN R.

YALU R.

Chosan

YALU R.

CHANGJIN
RESERVOIR

PUJON
RESERVOIR

Antung

YALU R.

Sinuiju

CHONGCHON R.

Anju

Hamhung

TAEDONG R.

Hungnam

NORTH
KOREA

Pyongyang

Wonsan

SEA OF JAPAN

TAEDONG R.

IMJIN R.

HWACHON
RESERVOIR

38°

38°

ONGJIN
PENINSULA

Chunchon

Inchon

Seoul

PUKHAN R.

HAN R.

T'AEBAEK RANGE

Suwon

Osan

Chungju

SOUTH
KOREA

1ST U.S. CONTACT
TASK FORCE SMITH

YELLOW
SEA

KUM R.

Taejon

NAKTONG R.

Kunsan

Taegu

Pohang

SOBAEK RANGE

NAM R.

PUSAN
PERIMETER

Pusan

KOJE-DO

PONGAM-DO

TSUSHIMA

HONSHU

0   Miles   100

Shimonoseki

palacias

CHEJU-DO

KYUSHU

action in the light of present knowledge and a resolution drafted for presentation to the UN Security Council. A talk with the President gave him the facts, secured his approval of the resolution, and instructed me to have the available people from State and Defense meet with him at Blair House, the temporary White House, that evening. Later a message from the plane added that the group should come to Blair House for dinner at seven-thirty. I left word at Defense for the Secretary and General Bradley, due back that afternoon, the service secretaries, and the Chiefs of Staff, and took with me Under Secretary James E. Webb, Assistant Secretaries Hickerson and Rusk, and Ambassador Jessup.

June 1950. The President had just rushed back from Missouri to Washington as the Korean crisis deepened. On his right is Secretary of Defense Louis Johnson. On his left, the author. INTERNATIONAL NEWS

An early draft of our resolution determined that the "armed attack on the Republic of Korea by forces from North Korea" constituted "an unprovoked act of aggression." When this draft was shown to some members of the Security Council, they expressed doubt whether the information yet available established the conclusion. They were, however, prepared to say that it "constituted a breach of the peace." Their preference for this statement was strengthened upon learning that our representative had not yet been instructed what our course would be should the North Koreans disregard the call for an immediate cessation of hostilities and a withdrawal of their forces to the 38th parallel as provided in the resolution. To meet these views the change was made.

When the Security Council convened on Sunday afternoon, it was not known whether Malik, the Soviet Representative, who was boycotting the council because of the presence of a Nationalist

Chinese and had returned to Moscow, would appear. He did not. There was no negative vote, and the resolution was declared adopted by a vote of 9–0, with Yugoslavia abstaining.[1] I met the President with the news at the airport and drove with him to Blair House.

During the afternoon I had everyone and all messages kept out of my room for an hour or two while I ruminated about the situation. "Thought," would suggest too orderly and purposeful a process. It was rather to let various possibilities, like glass fragments in a kaleidoscope, form a series of patterns of action and then draw conclusions from them. Our recommendations for the President dealt with the next twenty-four hours or so, which was as far as we could see at the time. But what must we contemplate beyond that? One possibility was that the attack would be called off; the other, that it would not be. For some months, as tensions had mounted again after the Berlin blockade, we had run exercises on danger spots for renewed Soviet probing of our determination. Korea was on the list but not among the favorites. Berlin, Turkey, Greece, Iran—all seemed spots where the balance of convenient operation dipped in favor of the Soviets. Korea was too near major forces and bases of ours in Japan and too far from any of theirs to offer a tempting target, though they could have judged our interest in it less than in the other places. But now the attack had come there. What was likely to happen next and how should we determine our

1. The text of the resolution was as follows:

The Security Council

Recalling the finding of the General Assembly in its resolution of 21 October 1949 that the Government of the Republic of Korea is a lawfully established government "having effective control and jurisdiction over that part of Korea where the United Nations Temporary Commission on Korea was able to observe and consult and in which the great majority of the people of Korea reside; and that this Government is based on elections which were a valid expression of the free will of the electorate of that part of Korea and which were observed by the Temporary Commission; and that this is the only such Government in Korea";

Mindful of the concern expressed by the General Assembly in its resolutions of 12 December 1948 and 21 October 1949 of the consequences which might follow unless Member states refrained from acts derogatory to the results sought to be achieved by the United Nations in bringing about the complete independence and unity of Korea; and the concern expressed that the situation described by the United Nations Commission on Korea in its report menaces the safety and well-being of the Republic of Korea and of the people of Korea and might lead to open military conflict there;

Noting with grave concern the armed attack upon the Republic of Korea by forces from North Korea,

Determines that this action constitutes a breach of the peace,

I. *Calls upon* the authorities of North Korea (a) to cease hostilities forthwith; and (b) to withdraw their armed forces to the thirty-eighth parallel.

II. *Requests* the United Nations Commission on Korea (a) to observe the withdrawal of the North Korean forces to the thirty-eighth parallel; and (b) to keep the Security Council informed on the execution of this resolution.

III. *Calls upon* all Members to render every assistance to the United Nations in the execution of this resolution and to refrain from giving assistance to the North Korean authorities.

Department of State Bulletin, Vol. XXIII, July 3, 1950, pp. 4–5.

response? It seemed close to certain that the attack had been mounted, supplied, and instigated by the Soviet Union and that it would not be stopped by anything short of force. If Korean force proved unequal to the job, as seemed probable, only American military intervention could do it. Troops from other sources would be helpful politically and psychologically but unimportant militarily.

Plainly, this attack did not amount to a *casus belli* against the Soviet Union. Equally plainly, it was an open, undisguised challenge to our internationally accepted position as the protector of South Korea, an area of great importance to the security of American-occupied Japan. To back away from this challenge, in view of our capacity for meeting it, would be highly destructive of the power and prestige of the United States. By prestige I mean the shadow cast by power, which is of great deterrent importance. Therefore, we could not accept the conquest of this important area by a Soviet puppet under the very guns of our defensive perimeter with no more resistance than words and gestures in the Security Council. It looked as though we must steel ourselves for the use of force. That did not mean, in words used later by General Mark Clark, that we must be prepared "to shoot the works for victory," but rather to see that the attack failed.

When I set off to meet the President, I had no plan, but my mind was pretty clear on where the course we were about to recommend would lead and why it was necessary that we follow that course.

The full group invited was assembled at Blair House. While waiting for dinner to be announced, Secretary Johnson asked General Bradley to read a memorandum that he had brought from General Douglas MacArthur on the strategic importance of Formosa. I recognized this as an opening gun in a diversionary argument that Johnson wished to start with me. Evidently another did also, for when General Bradley had finished, the President announced that discussion of the Far Eastern situation had better be postponed until after dinner when we would be alone. The subject was thereupon dropped and conversation was kept to general topics. After dinner the President asked me to report the latest developments and any recommendations the two departments had prepared for him. I gave a darkening report of great confusion and read three recommendations:

1. General MacArthur should be authorized and directed to supply Korea with arms and other equipment over and above that already allocated under the Military Assistance Program.

2. The U.S. Air Force should be ordered to protect Kimpo

airport during the evacuation of United States dependents by attacking any North Korean ground or air forces approaching it.

3. The Seventh Fleet should be ordered to proceed from the Philippines north and to prevent any attack from China on Formosa or vice versa.

I also urged that military assistance to Indochina be stepped up.

Each person around the room was then asked for his views. The recommendations were supported with varying degrees of detail. There was quite general uniformity of view that the occasion called for prompt and vigorous action as it became clearer. The President discussed with the soldiers the likelihood of the Soviet Union's pushing the crisis to general war. The consensus was to the contrary, since the military balance was more favorable to the United States and unfavorable to the Soviet Union than it was likely to continue in the longer run. They were not in favor of using ground forces under conditions then existing. General J. Lawton Collins pressed for and obtained the President's authority to have General MacArthur send a survey team to Korea to make a first-hand appraisal and report.

At the end, about eleven o'clock, the President accepted my recommendations, although reserving decision on what orders to issue to the Seventh Fleet until it should reach the Formosa Straits about thirty-six hours later and be able to carry them out. He also added two instructions of his own to me—to make a survey of other likely spots for Soviet strikes and to prepare a statement for him to make on Tuesday (perhaps to Congress) reporting what had been done. He said that he wanted the Department's best brains put to work on these tasks and added that "there are plenty of them there." These were the most cheering words from a President to or about the State Department in years. Before we broke up, he emphasized that no statement whatever was to be made by anyone until he spoke on Tuesday. There must be no leaks, not even background statements to the press. I reminded him that Louis Johnson and I had to appear before the Senate Appropriations Committee on Monday. Nevertheless, he said, no statements on Korea were to be made by either of us.

At the end of the meeting I showed the President a message from John Foster Dulles, who in April had been appointed a consultant to the Department of State and charged with the preparation of the Japanese peace treaty, in connection with which he had gone to the Far East. Returning to Tokyo from a visit to Korea, he reported: "It is possible that South Koreans may themselves contain and repulse attack, and, if so, this is the best way. If, however, it appears that they cannot do so then we believe that US force should be used even though this risks Russian countermoves. To sit by while Korea is overrun by unprovoked armed attack would start disastrous chain of events leading most probably to world war. We suggest that Security Council might call for action." [2]

Monday, June 26

A day of steadily worsening reports from Korea, but work went on. Assignments were made to carry out the President's instructions of the preceding evening. I went over my testimony for the Appropriations Committee, and then spent half an hour telephoning Senators Tom Connally and Alexander Wiley and Judge John Kee of the House committee, repeating what was in the press; reporting our support for the United Nations, whose representatives were busy in Korea; and asking that any meeting with congressional committees be held off for a day, "until we had some hard information to report." The appropriations hearing went off without too much trouble.

On my return the news was much worse. More calls from and to the Capitol; finally Assistant Secretary Jack McFall went up to prepare the chairmen for what appeared a growing rout. After lunch the Korean Ambassador, distraught and weeping, called on the President with me to present South Korean President Syngman Rhee's plea for help. The President soothed him, and I gave him a statement to read as he went out which assured him that we were solidly backing the United Nations.

Returning to the Department, I conferred with those who had been working on the President's assignments. What followed is recorded in a minute by one of those present: "The Secretary broke off the discussions we had been having with him and said that he wanted to be alone and to dictate. We were called in about 6:30 P.M. and he read to us a paper he had produced, which was a first draft of the statement finally issued by the President, and which was not significantly changed by the time it appeared the following day."

After dinner downtown and further conferences with State and Defense officers, I telephoned the President that the situation in Korea was becoming so desperate that he would wish to hear about it firsthand and instruct us further. He summoned the same group

2. Harry S. Truman, *Years of Trial and Hope,* Vol. II, *Memoirs* (New York: Doubleday & Company, 1956), p. 336.

to Blair House which had met there on Sunday.

It met there at nine o'clock, Deputy Under Secretary H. Freeman Matthews taking Webb's place. General Hoyt S. Vandenberg reported that a Russian plane had been shot down by our forces and that the South Koreans were breaking all along the front under a formidable attack. In response to the President's request for suggestions, I recommended that:

1. The Air Force and Navy should give all-out support to the Korean forces, for the time being confining their efforts to south of the 38th parallel.

2. The Seventh Fleet should be ordered to prevent an attack on Formosa, the Nationalists told not to attack the mainland, and the Fleet told to prevent their doing so, if necessary.

3. U.S. forces in the Philippines should be strengthened and aid to Philippine forces accelerated.

4. Aid to Indochina should be increased and we should propose to the French that we send a strong military mission.

5. If the President approved the foregoing, he should issue the statement I had prepared as directed and which included actions recommended.

6. At the Security Council meeting called for the next morning we should propose a new resolution (which Hickerson read) calling on UN members to give Korea such help as might be needed to repel the armed attack and restore peace in the area. If Malik returned to the Security Council and vetoed the resolution, we would have to carry on under the existing one. If he did not return, it would pass without opposition.

We had speculated a great deal about the probable Soviet move. The uncertainty about it added one more element of chance to the puzzle before us. Charles Bohlen and George Kennan, who spoke with most experience on the subject, believed that the cumbersome Soviet bureaucracy was simply not equipped to make quick decisions. It would take some time, they thought, for Moscow to figure out the correlation of forces involved. The betting was against the presence of a Russian at the Security Council meeting on the morrow.

The recommendations met with general favor, including Louis Johnson's, and were approved by the President. The Army officers present doubted whether naval and air support could save the Korean forces, though the Navy and Air Force view was more optimistic. If it became necessary to commit ground forces in Korea, they thought some degree of mobilization might become necessary. The President asked that this be given immediate study.

He then raised the question of consultation with congressional leaders. After some discussion Secretary Johnson and I were directed to meet with him at the White House the next morning to talk with the Speaker—the Vice President would be away—the majority leaders, Senator Scott Lucas (Ill.) and Representative John Mc-Cormack (Mass.); Senators Tom Connally (Tex.), Walter George (Ga.), and Elbert Thomas (Utah), Democrats, and Alexander Wiley (Wis.) and Alexander Smith (N.J.), Republicans, from the Foreign Relations Committee, and Millard Tydings (Md.) and Styles Bridges (N.H.) from the Armed Services Committee; Congressmen John Kee (W.Va.), Mike Mansfield (Mont.), and Charles Eaton (N.J.) of Foreign Affairs and Carl Vinson (Ga.) and Dewey Short (Mo.) of Armed Services.

Orders to carry out the decisions of Monday evening issued at once and were immediately obeyed. The UN Security Council meeting set for Tuesday morning was postponed until the afternoon to enable the Indian representative to receive instruction. Thus some American action, said to be in support of the resolution of June 27, was in fact ordered, and possibly taken, prior to the resolution. Later on, Russian propaganda attempted to play this up, but the effort received the attention it deserved.

Tuesday, June 27

At the President's meeting with the congressional leaders, Assistant Secretaries Matthews, Rusk, and Hickerson and Ambassador Jessup accompanied me. The Chiefs of Staff and service secretaries came with Secretary Johnson. The meeting was held in the Cabinet Room, Johnson and I flanking the President, with the legislators around the table and the others behind them. The President asked me to summarize the situation, and then stressed the prompt action of the Security Council, read the statement, later published,[3] of the orders he had already issued, and reported our efforts to communicate with the Soviet Government. He then asked for views. Various questions about military dispositions were answered by the Chiefs, including the fact that no ground forces had yet been committed. Senator Wiley seemed to express the consensus by saying that it was enough for him to know that we were in there with force and that the President thought the force adequate. Senator Tydings reported that his committee had that morning recommended an extension of the draft act and presidential authority to call out the National Guard.

3. *Department of State Bulletin*, Vol. XXIII, July 3, 1950, p. 5.

Questions having turned to the political field, the President stated that our actions were taken in support of the United Nations efforts to restore peace in the area. In regard to Formosa, however, his orders were ancillary, aimed at preventing any new outbreak of fighting. I discussed the proposed Security Council resolution, ventured the opinion that Malik would not attend the meeting, and pointed out that since the USSR had not yet publicly committed itself we were careful not to engage Soviet prestige at this time. Congressman Eaton inquired whether the United States was now committed to defend South Korea. The President answered yes, as a member of the United Nations and in response to the Security Council's resolutions. Asked about help from other nations, I replied that not much could be expected since others either had their hands full, like the French, or had little to spare. After assurance that Congress would be kept currently informed of developments and general agreement that release of the President's statement would make separate comments unnecessary, the meeting broke up.

While we were talking the Security Council met, without Malik, and adopted the United States resolution, with Yugoslavia dissenting and Egypt and India abstaining.

President Truman's statement [4] referring to the continuance of the North Korean attack despite the UN call for its cessation said: "In these circumstances, I have ordered United States air and sea forces to give the Korean Government troops cover and support." It added that an attack on Formosa under these circumstances would be a direct threat to the security of the Pacific area and to United States forces performing their lawful and necessary functions there. "Accordingly," the President's statement continued, "I have ordered the Seventh Fleet to prevent any attack on Formosa. As a corollary of this action, I am calling upon the Chinese Government on Formosa to cease all air and sea operations against the mainland. The Seventh Fleet will see that this is done." The statement also recited the other actions that had been taken.

Later the same day we told the press of our note to the Soviet Union. In view of their Representative's refusal to attend the Security Council's meeting and of their close relations with the North Korean authorities, we were approaching them directly, we said, to ask their disavowal of responsibility for the attack and the use of their influence with the North Koreans "for withdrawal of the invading forces and cessation of hostilities." On the twenty-ninth they replied that the attack had been made by the South Koreans and responsibility for its consequences rested upon them

4. *Ibid.*

"and upon those who stand behind their back." [5]

On Tuesday Governor Thomas E. Dewey of New York read to me over the telephone a statement giving his support to the Administration's action on Korea and asked for suggestions. I welcomed it with warmest appreciation and gratitude. He released it at once.

Wednesday, June 28

Immediately following Governor Dewey's support, Senator Robert A. Taft opened up in the Senate. His speech was typical—bitterly partisan and ungracious, but basically honest. The Administration was responsible, he said, for the trouble that had overtaken it. The division of Korea, failure to arm the South sufficiently, the "loss of China" to the Communists, my "invitation to attack" in the January 12 speech, had all made attack inevitable. Even now the President had done the right thing in the wrong way. The Senator would have approved a congressional resolution authorizing intervention but doubted the constitutionality of the President's executive action. The ground Senator Taft chose was typical senatorial legalistic ground for differing with the President. As a result, discussion in Congress of these differences is singularly lacking in understanding of substantive issues. When it escapes the shackles of the separation of powers, it is apt to bog down in the moral shortcomings of those foreign governments with whom the United States is cooperating. They are usually said to be lacking either in energetic action for the common cause or in moral fervor for democratic doctrines.

Of much greater importance to me than Senator Taft's opposition was W. Averell Harriman's return to Washington. For some time he had wished to return, as he believed that his work in Paris for the Marshall Plan had largely been accomplished. Washington was the center of the world; he felt isolated in Europe. I had been working with and on the President to bring Averell back. To find a place for him was not an easy task. Averell had immense prestige and was aware of it. Many were jealous of him. No one would wish to stand aside. Washington is like a self-sealing tank on military aircraft: when a bullet passes through, it closes up. Averell, the President agreed, could be immensely useful in smoothing out Cabinet relations on foreign affairs, especially with Defense. However, he warned me that should Harriman return to do this the

5. *Ibid.*, and July 10, pp. 47–48.

press would have it that he was slated to succeed me and that long knives would be whetted to speed fulfillment of the prophecy. The fact that there would be gossip, I agreed, was of course true, but the President, Averell, and I would know that there was no truth in it. My forty-five years of confidence in Averell's integrity and honor would not be undermined by those whom Lincoln called "the scribblers."

Therefore, at a press conference on June 16, I had "warmly welcomed" word from the White House of Averell's impending appointment as Special Assistant to the President. The need for it had long been felt. So far as I was concerned there could not have been a happier choice. The President had worked it out after consultation with Mr. Harriman and me. Since 1905, I said, "which, perhaps, some of you don't remember, . . . we have been close friends and worked together at all sorts of things."

On Tuesday morning, June 27, Averell had telephoned me from Paris, carried away with enthusiasm about the President's action about Korea. He could not stand delaying his return another hour while Washington was electrifying the world. He would leave at once, counting on me to "square it with the boss." From that time on, through all the period we were in the Government together, he attended our nine-thirty meeting in the Department almost every day, and any other meeting he wished, read all the important cables, and had access to all information. The direst predictions of trouble to come and the greatest efforts to sow it were made without the slightest effect. Averell's loyal help and wise advice were invaluable to the President, to me, and to the whole Administration.

At the National Security Council meeting on the afternoon of the twenty-eighth I pointed out that we could not count on the continuance of the enthusiastic support that our staunch attitude in Korea had evoked in the country and in the world. Firm leadership would be less popular if it should involve casualties and taxes. The President, mistaking my purpose, which was to prepare for criticism and hard sledding, insisted that we could not back out of the course upon which we had started. The reply was typical of one of his most admirable traits. He was unmoved by, indeed unmindful of, the effect upon his or his party's political fortunes of action that he thought was right and in the best interest of the country, broadly conceived. A doctrine that later became fashionable with presidents, called "keeping all options open" (apparently by avoiding decision), did not appeal to Harry S. Truman.

Thursday, June 29

Wednesday had been a day of pause in the rush of decisions. On Thursday it picked up again. Brigadier General John Church, who had been sent to Korea by General MacArthur to report the situation, had signaled that the *status quo ante* could not be restored without the commitment of United States troops, and by Thursday morning the news was much worse. All attempts to halt the South Korean retreat at the Han River south of Seoul failed. By noon the gloom deepened. The President called a meeting of the "Blair House Group" for five o'clock.

Decisions at this meeting increased the involvement of our air and naval forces to include military targets in North Korea, but not beyond, and authorized the use of ground forces to secure the port, airfield, and communications facilities at Pusan, considerably south of the combat zone. Meanwhile General MacArthur had gone by plane from Tokyo to make his own reconnaisance at the scene of the fighting. He was told that should Soviet forces intervene he was to provide for the security of his own troops and report at once to Washington. However, as I have already suggested, it was State's view that while the Chinese might intervene, the Russians would not.

Shortly after this meeting I returned to the White House with an offer by Generalissimo Chiang Kai-shek to contribute thirty-three thousand troops to the Korean action, to be transported and supplied by the United States. The President seemed to look with favor on this idea, which I argued against on the grounds that these troops would be more useful defending Formosa than Korea. He directed me to bring it up the next day before the full group, when he could hear all views.

Friday, June 30

General MacArthur, back in Tokyo after a hazardous expedition to the front in Korea, telegraphed General Collins, Chief of Staff of the Army, that the Korean retreat was a rout and that American combat troops were necessary to stop it. He asked for authority to send from Japan at once a regimental combat team as the spearhead of a two-division buildup as soon as possible afterward. This message came to Collins at three o'clock Friday morning and was immediately followed by a telecon discussion by General Collins, Secretary of the Army Pace, and Assistant Secretary of

State Rusk at the Pentagon with General MacArthur in Tokyo. (A telecon is a secure device by which a typewriter operated at one end records both there and through a similar machine at the other end.) General MacArthur elaborated his telegraphed report, underlining the urgent need for American military help at the front.

Secretary Pace telephoned the President at five o'clock, finding him up and dressing for his morning walk. The President immediately granted authority to move the augmented regiment, promised a further reply in a few hours, and ordered a meeting of the Blair House Group at the White House at eight-thirty that morning. Rusk filled me in on the way to the meeting. The request from the front and the President's response came as no surprise to me.

At the White House the President informed us of what he had already done and asked for advice regarding the next step. He spoke favorably of Chiang's offer of troops immediately available. I opposed the latter on the grounds that the net result might well be the reverse of helpful by bringing Chinese Communist intervention, either in Korea or Formosa or both. The Chiefs of Staff sided with me, saying that the transport could better be used for our own troops and supplies, since Chiang's best troops were not likely to be of much help against the North Korean armor. The unanimous advice of the group was to follow the force already authorized with the two divisions from Japan. The President so decided and approved the necessary orders.

The decision not to accept the Generalissimo's offer brought from General MacArthur the suggestion that he go to Formosa to explain it. Instinct told us what experience later proved—to fear General MacArthur bearing explanations. Furthermore, better uses for the theater commander at this juncture came to mind, so a State Department officer was sent from Tokyo to Formosa with the explanation.

At eleven o'clock I returned to the White House for a meeting with congressional leaders, taking Foster Dulles, just back from Tokyo, with me. The congressional group was perhaps twice as large as the one at the Tuesday meeting. The President reported the situation in Korea, reviewed the actions previously taken by the United Nations Security Council and the United States Government, and the orders he had issued that morning. A general chorus of approval was interrupted by, I think, Senator Kenneth Wherry (Neb.) questioning the legal authority of the executive to take this action. Senator Alexander Smith suggested a congressional resolution approving the President's action. The President said that he would consider Smith's suggestion and asked me to prepare a

In late June, John Foster Dulles reported to the White House on his return from Korea and Japan. On his right, General J. Lawton Collins, Army Chief of Staff. On his left, the author, and General Omar Bradley. WIDE WORLD

Leaving the White House Conference, at which it was decided to go all out to defend South Korea. Left to right, the author, Ambassador Philip Jessup, and Assistant Secretary of State Dean Rusk. WIDE WORLD

recommendation. The meeting ended with Representative Dewey Short stating that Congress was practically unanimous in its appreciation of the President's leadership. Short was a Republican from the President's home state of Missouri and ranking minority member of the Armed Services Committee.

Friday's decisions were the culminating ones of a momentous week. We were then fully committed in Korea.

II

THE FIRST CRISIS

An Anxious Summer

IN THE DAYS that followed I considered Senator Alexander Smith's suggestion, and on July 3 the President assembled a group at Blair House to hear and discuss my recommendation. Jessup and Rusk went with me. Secretary Johnson brought the service secretaries and General Bradley. The President had with him Secretaries John W. Snyder of the Treasury and Charles F. Brannan of Agriculture; Postmaster General Jesse M. Donaldson; Senate Majority Leader Scott W. Lucas; and Averell Harriman.

My recommendation was that the President make a full report on the Korean situation to a joint session of Congress. This would, of course, be largely formal but would bring the whole story together in one official narrative and meet the objection of some members that information had come to them only through the leaders and the press. I also recommended that the President should not ask for a resolution of approval, but rest on his constitutional authority as Commander in Chief of the armed forces. However, we had drafted a resolution commending the action taken by the United States that would be acceptable if proposed by members of Congress.

In the ensuing discussion it appeared that the two houses of Congress had just recessed for a week and the President was unwilling to call them back. Senator Lucas, General Bradley, and Secretary Johnson were opposed to both recommendations: to the report because it would come too long after the events to stand by itself and had better accompany a request for money and necessary powers; and to the resolution because the vast majority in Congress were satisfied and the irreconcilable minority could not be won over. They could, however, keep debating and delaying a resolution so as to dilute much of its public effect. The others were divided. My sympathies lay with the Lucas-Bradley view. So apparently did the President's, for he put off a decision until the "Big Four" (the presiding officers and majority leaders of both houses) would be back after the recess. By then we were pretty well won over to Senator Lucas' view.

There has never, I believe, been any serious doubt—in the sense of non-politically inspired doubt—of the President's constitutional authority to do what he did. The basis for this conclusion in legal theory and historical precedent was fully set out in the State Department's memorandum of July 3, 1950, extensively published.[1] But the wisdom of the decision not to ask for congressional approval has been doubted. To have obtained congressional approval, it has been argued, would have obviated later criticism of "Truman's war." In my opinion, it would have changed pejorative phrases, but little else. Congressional approval did not soften or divert the antiwar critics of Presidents Lincoln, Wilson, and Roosevelt. What inspired the later criticism of the Korean war was the long, hard struggle, casualties, cost, frustration of a limited and apparently inconclusive war, and—most of all—the determination of the opposition to end seemingly interminable Democratic rule.

Nevertheless, it is said, congressional approval would have done no harm. True, approval would have done none, but the process of gaining it might well have done a great deal. July—and especially the first part of it—was a time of anguishing anxiety. As American troops were committed to battle, they and their Korean allies under brutal punishment staggered back down the peninsula until they maintained only a precarious hold on the coastal perimeter around Pusan. An incredulous country and world held its breath and read the mounting casualties suffered by these gallant troops, most of them without combat experience. In the confusion of the retreat even their divisional commander, Major General William F. Dean, was captured. Congressional hearings on a resolution of approval at such a time, opening the possibility of endless criticism, would hardly be calculated to support the shaken morale of the troops or the unity that, for the moment, prevailed at home. The harm it could do seemed to me far to outweigh the little good that might ultimately accrue.

The President agreed, moved also, I think, by another passionately held conviction. His great office was to him a sacred and temporary trust, which he was determined to pass on unim-

1. *Department of State Bulletin*, Vol. XXIII, July 31, 1950, pp. 173–78.

paired by the slightest loss of power or prestige. This attitude would incline him strongly against any attempt to divert criticism from himself by action that might establish a precedent in derogation of presidential power to send our forces into battle. The memorandum that we prepared listed eighty-seven instances in the past century in which his predecessors had done this. And thus yet another decision was made.

Shortly after the seven days of June just described a paper came to me from the White House. I end this account with it, partly and unquestionably from pride, but also because it illustrates so well a quality of the President's that bound his lieutenants to him with unbreakable devotion. The paper was a longhand note:

Memo to Dean Acheson
Regarding June 24 and 25—   7/19/50
Your initiative in immediately calling the Security Council of the U.N. on Saturday night and notifying me was the key to what followed afterwards. Had you not acted promptly in that direction we would have had to go into Korea alone.

The meeting Sunday night at the Blair House was the result of your action Saturday night and the results afterward show that you are a great Secretary of State and a diplomat.

Your handling of the situation since has been superb.

I'm sending you this for your record.

Harry S. Truman

After the seven days of decision my work was less heavily concentrated on Korean matters though still continuously involved with them. The attack helped to activate other problems that crowded anxious days—the battle with the Republican "irreconcilables," to use a phrase common just thirty years earlier, and the concern and fear of our European allies that our absorption in the desperate battle going on in Korea might dilute our attention to their security.

From the very start of hostilities in Korea, President Truman intended to fight a limited engagement there. In this determination he had the staunch and unwavering support of the State and Defense departments and the Joint Chiefs of Staff. Such a war policy requires quite as much determination as any other kind. It also calls for restraint and fine judgment, a sure sense of how far is far enough; it may involve, as it did in Korea, a great deal of frustration. In its execution, this policy invites dissent and criticism both from those who are afraid that the balance is being tipped against the possibility of keeping the war limited and from those who fear that keeping it limited precludes the possibility of victory and who believe that "there is no substitute for victory." The former, now called "doves," reduce the national objective with every reversal and soon wish to scrap the whole effort. The "hawks" would raise the sights with every success and call for unconditional surrender. Prominent, even in this early period, among the former were the British and the Indians, joined later on by the Canadians, and among the latter General MacArthur and the congressional advocates of a "hard China policy," especially the irreconcilable Republicans.

Anglo-Indian Peace Initiatives

The British Foreign Office had long believed, more than evidence seemed to warrant, that it understood the Russians and could negotiate with them compromise solutions of difficult situations. To others, the proposed compromises often resembled surrenders. In July, while our troops were fighting against heavy odds to keep a toehold in Korea, we found ourselves engaged in a month of discussion of their unsolicited initiative to bring about a "peaceful settlement" there. Independently, and unknown to the British, the Indians had started an effort of their own. My comment about British diplomacy vis-à-vis the Soviet Union would be quite inadequate to describe the Indian variety.

Immediately after the June 27 resolution of the Security Council, the British Government helpfully and loyally put British warships in Japanese waters at General MacArthur's disposal as the quickest method of furnishing help to Korea. Later they sent the heroic brigade of "The Glosters," which fought and suffered so gallantly. Almost at once His Majesty's Government also began its search for a peaceful settlement. In early July Sir David Kelly, British Ambassador to the Soviet Union, was trying to get in touch with Deputy Foreign Minister Andrei A. Gromyko, and Prime Minister Clement R. Attlee proposed to the President talks in Washington between presidential nominees and Air Marshal Lord Arthur Tedder and British Ambassador to the United States Oliver Franks. I suggested that Ambassador Philip Jessup join General Omar Bradley, the President's choice from the services.

At the same time, Ambassador Alan G. Kirk reported from Moscow that Gromyko had asked Kelly whether he had any specific proposal for a peaceful settlement, and that Kelly had replied, "The *status quo ante*." Ambassador Kirk urged that we make clear to the British—who had meanwhile told us that further talks in Moscow would come only after full discussion with us—that a prerequisite for peaceful settlement was complete compliance by North Korea with the Security Council's call for a cease-fire and withdrawal of the invading forces north of the 38th parallel.

Ambassador Kirk had been a close friend for thirty years. He had commanded the United States Naval force that had put our army ashore in Sicily in 1943 and on the Normandy beaches in 1944. Well-known in Europe and knowledgeable about it, he outstandingly possessed the qualities of courage and good sense which the President sought in a successor to our Ambassador in Moscow (former General and Chief of Staff to General Eisenhower in North Africa and Europe) Walter Bedell Smith. At this particular turn in events, Kirk's lack of Russian was not an important drawback. Stalin was not a gossipy type; Vishinsky did not count; and Gromyko was walking on eggs. What we would expect of the Ambassador would not be brilliant suggestions on how to solve the Russian enigma but immediate and firm execution of his instructions, full reporting, and careful, solicitous attention to the condition and morale of the mission, beleaguered as it was and subject to traps and pressures.

On July 7, our attitude toward admitting the Chinese Communists to the United Nations having hardened since the outbreak of the Korean hostilities, I sent an instruction to Ambassador Lewis Douglas in London to say to Ernest Bevin, the British Foreign Minister, or to Kenneth Younger, British Minister of State, that we thought the Kelly-Gromyko talks might be useful if restricted solely to finding out what, if anything, Moscow had in mind; that we were not willing to bargain any positions in exchange for an end to the aggression. The British might also suggest the feasibility of the USSR's using its influence with the North Koreans to accept the three specific points of the UN June 25 resolution. The Ambassador garnered the information that a group in the Foreign Office, described as "influential," were, indeed, eager to get the Chinese Communists into the United Nations as soon as possible to frustrate a supposed Russian desire to isolate China from the West.

Crossing the Department's instruction to Douglas was a letter of July 7 from Bevin, transmitted to me by Ambassador Franks on July 8. Bevin wrote of his belief that the Kremlin really wished to restore the *status quo ante*, but he believed they would link a change in our position on Formosa with it. That position, he said, did not have the backing of the states that supported the UN Korean resolutions. We should avoid risking Western solidarity by playing down those parts of the President's statement of June

27 that did not bear directly on Korea.

One can easily imagine that this message did not please either the President or me. I therefore drafted and he approved a frank reply, dated July 10, 1950, which, indicating its joint authorship, made four points:

1. We would not agree to a forced trade of Formosa to the Communists for their withdrawal from Korea.

2. Our policy aimed at as early and complete a liquidation of the Korean aggression as was militarily possible, without concessions that would whet Communists appetites and bring on other aggressions elsewhere.

3. It also aimed at the peaceful disposition of the Formosan question, either in a peace treaty with Japan or through the United Nations.

4. If questions regarding Formosa or the representation of China in the United Nations were to be considered there, we regarded it essential that they be considered on their merits and not under the duress and blackmail then being employed.

Our Ambassador was also instructed to stress orally the undesirability of the British agitating in the present situation that China be represented on the Security Council by the Communist regime or that Malik return to it. He was to say, also, that both the President and I took a serious view of Mr. Bevin's note and the portent that its contents carried for future Anglo-American cooperation.

The Ambassador, who delivered this letter to Bevin in the hospital on July 11, found him taken aback by its vigor and defensive in explaining his own position. Bevin's written reply warned that we must not drive China into Soviet hands, and stated that although aggression must be repelled and he would not yield to blackmail, he wanted the Soviet Union and the Communist Chinese in the Security Council. The correspondence clearly had no future, so we dropped it.

The Tedder-Bradley talks also added nothing. General Bradley explained that some weeks would be needed to build our strength to a point where it would tell decisively. The Russians, he thought, would not intervene overtly, for that would mean war, and such a war would not be fought in Korea.

Meanwhile, the Indian initiative for peaceful settlement was gathering momentum in multisplendored confusion. In Moscow Indian Ambassador Sarvepalli Radhakrishnan approached Deputy Foreign Minister Valerian Zorin; in Washington Mme. Pandit, Indian Ambassador and Nehru's sister, talked to me; in India Sir Girja Bajpai, Secretary General of the Foreign Office, spoke to U.S.

Ambassador Loy Henderson; and in the United Nations Krishna
Menon took on our people. Each presented the scheme a little
differently and insisted that the effort must be kept secret from the
British, which, of course, was not done. The general idea was that
we were to support seating the Communist Chinese on the Security
Council, which would then, with the Russians and Chinese Communists both on it, support a cease-fire, withdrawal of North Korean
troops to the 38th parallel, and the re-creation of a unified and
independent Korea.

On July 11 Kirk learned via Radhakrishnan that Gromyko had
rejected the second part of the proposal out of hand. With the
President's approval, Kirk was authorized to tell his Indian colleague
that we would agree to nothing that rewarded an aggressor, diluted
the requirements of the June 25 and 27 resolutions of the Security
Council, or left Korea after hostilities in an exposed and defenseless
situation.

Then, on July 13, Prime Minister Nehru sent personal letters
to Stalin and to me making a proposal even less satisfactory to us
than the one rejected in Moscow.[2] India's purpose, he wrote, was
to localize the conflict and to facilitate an early peaceful settlement
by breaking the present deadlock in the Security Council so that
Communist Chinese representatives could take a seat there, the
Russians could return to it, and, either within or outside the council, the United States, the Soviet Union, and China, with the
help and cooperation of other peace-loving nations, could find a
basis for terminating the conflict and for a permanent solution of
the Korean problem. In this endeavor the Prime Minister wished
to enlist my great authority and influence.

Although the logic of this proposal was obscure—to seat the
Communists in the Security Council in order to permit informal
contacts outside it—the effect was abundantly clear. It would
transfer the center of attention and discussion from the aggression
in Korea to who should represent China on the Security Council.
The ousting of the Nationalists from the council—for that was the
essence of the matter—was to be the price for the privilege of opening discussion about North Korean troop withdrawal. The next in-
stallment, clearly forecast by Bajpai to Henderson, would be the
ousting of the Nationalists from Formosa. Meanwhile our troops
would be fighting a rear-guard action down the peninsula of Korea
as the Communists tried to drive them out of it. I felt no need for
advice in making up my mind on such a proposal. However, I was

2. *Ibid.,* p. 170.

to receive spiritual exhortation.

Mme. Vijaya Lakshmi Pandit—a most charming lady—called on me on July 17 with an appeal from her brother. Apprehension that Peking's entry into the Security Council and Moscow's return might possibly lead to obstruction should not delay restoration of the council's full representative character. Insistence upon prior conditions—such as the return of North Koreans to the 38th parallel—would be used as evidence of a lack of desire on our part for peaceful settlement (sic!). If after taking their seats the Chinese should be unreasonable, world opinion would hold them responsible. Moscow, her brother thought, was seeking a way out; here was the real path to peaceful settlement. "It may be an act of faith, but the gravity of the alternatives seems to justify it," she said. I have never been able to escape wholly from a childhood illusion that, if the world is round, the Indians must be standing on their heads—or, perhaps, vice versa.

With the President's approval, I replied on July 18, trying to put first things first. The key paragraph stated: "A breach of the peace or an act of aggression is the most serious matter with which the United Nations can be confronted. We do not believe that the termination of the aggression from northern Korea can be contingent in any way upon the determination of other questions which are currently before the United Nations." [3]

This letter was said to have annoyed Mr. Nehru. The correspondence, however, continued through one more repetitious exchange, which led Bajpai, a pleasant little man, to report severely to Henderson of Nehru's hope that the United States did not prefer a United Nations without the Soviet bloc. Two days later Moscow announced Malik's return to the Security Council, which happily ended India's initiative, for it would have been hard to argue that the Russians would not return to the council without the Chinese Communists after they had, in fact, returned.

Other nations responded to the UN resolutions with contributions more helpful than fanciful peace proposals. By the end of the year fifteen members had armed forces in Korea or on the way and thirty had contributed to civilian relief and reconstruction. By the middle of the month, with the battle still going against us as we fell back on Pusan, the Administration resumed with new urgency the examination begun in the winter and spring of our own and our allies' military posture.

3. *Ibid.*, pp. 170–71.

Arms and the Men

The dispatch of the two divisions to Korea removed the recommendations of the National Security Council document, NSC-
68, from the realm of theory and made them immediate budget
issues.[4] In the State Department, therefore, we were distressed by
the relaxed view of affairs taken by the Council of Economic Advisers in their midyear report, which assumed that fighting would
be kept localized and concluded that no stand-by economic control
powers were necessary. In our discussion we were unanimous in
agreeing that not only what the country did but what it was obviously preparing itself to do, if necessary, would greatly affect what
it might be called upon to do. We believed that the recommendations were totally inadequate and that opinion in the country was
prepared for vigorous action. Assistant Secretary for Economic
Affairs Willard Thorp was directed to express these views at White
House meetings on economic matters and arrange for my attendance
at them.

A report at a Cabinet meeting on July 14, which the President
had asked from State and Defense on possible future Soviet action,
gave an opportunity to raise the matter. We had concluded that
the Soviet Union had the military capability of taking action, directly or through satellites, at one or more points along its periphery
or of engaging in more general war. After suggesting places and
causes for trouble, I reported that unanimity did not exist on the
most probable spot or spots that might be chosen, but it did
exist on the extreme danger of some such action flowing from either
Soviet desire or the momentum of events. Any one or more of these
outbreaks would call for the use of more military power than we
could then deploy. I urged that the President ask for an immediate
increase in authorized forces of all services, for substantial appropriations—too much rather than too little—for increased military
production and powers to allocate and limit uses of raw materials,

4. For a discussion of the purpose, drafting, and recommendations of NSC–68,
see *Present at the Creation*, pp. 373–80. NSC–68 has not been declassified, but its
contents have been widely discussed in print. To meet the threat presented by the
conflicting aims and purposes of the two superpowers—the priority given by the Soviet
rulers to world domination and the American aim of an environment in which free
societies could exist and flourish—the paper recommended specific measures for a large
and immediate improvement of our military forces and weapons and of the economic
and morale factors underlying our own and our allies' ability to repair our weaknesses
and create situations of strength that could lead to useful negotiation with the
Russians. It seemed doubtful that without the courses recommended we would continue to be the stronger society. While the Russians put half their total effort into
creating miliary power, our air force no longer had a monopoly of atomic weapons;
our army had been demobilized and our navy put in mothballs.

and state that this was to increase the capabilities not only of our own forces but of allied forces as well.

The President agreed with all of this. Five days later he reported to Congress:

> Under all the circumstances, it is apparent that the United States is required to increase its military strength and preparedness not only to deal with the aggression in Korea but also to increase our common defense, with other free nations, against further aggression.
>
> The increased strength which is needed falls into three categories.
>
> In the first place, to meet the situation in Korea, we shall need to send additional men, equipment and supplies to General MacArthur's command as rapidly as possible.
>
> In the second place, the world situation requires that we increase substantially the size and materiel support of our armed forces, over and above the increases which are needed in Korea.
>
> In the third place, we must assist the free nations associated with us in common defense to augment their military strength.[5]

Appropriations and powers tumbled over one another, sometimes in such haste that supplemental appropriations virtually accompanied the regular fiscal-year bill they were supplementing. Thus in July the President signed fiscal year 1950–51 appropriations for mutual defense assistance of one billion two hundred million dollars and another four-billion-dollar supplemental appropriation in September. In August measures were taken to double the size of the armed forces. On September 6 the pre-existing Defense appropriation of fourteen billion six hundred million dollars was signed and on the twenty-seventh another twelve billion six hundred million added. In the meanwhile some export controls were obtained, and the National Defense Production Act, approved by the President on September 8, 1950, gave him some powers over the economic life of the country. But the economic control side of the program had been weakened under the powerful influence of Speaker Rayburn. This proved later to have been a mistake. Nevertheless, the country moved swiftly if in a somewhat disorderly way into a more formidable military posture.

It was often said that the Truman Administration and, particularly, the Secretary of State were "unpopular" and had trouble with Congress. It is true that many uncomplimentary things were said, but in Washington it is better to get what one wants than to be loved.

---

5. *Public Papers of the Presidents of the United States: Harry S. Truman, 1950* (Washington, D.C.: U.S. Government Printing Office, 1965), p. 532.

July 1950. The Korean crisis enveloped the government. Surrounding President Truman, whose back is eloquent of the man, are, from left to right, Secretary of Agriculture Brannan, Postmaster General Donaldson, the author, Secretary of the Interior Chapman, and Secretary of Defense Johnson. NEW YORK TIMES

MacArthur Drops Some Bricks

Before 1950 General MacArthur had neither shown nor expressed interest in Formosa. In discussing "our line of defense . . . against Asiatic aggression" with the press on March 1, 1949, he did not include that island.[6] But the General was not deaf to political reports coming to him from the United States, particularly those emanating from the Republican right wing, which found our Far

6. *The New York Times,* March 2, 1949, quoted General MacArthur as follows:
Our defensive dispositions against Asiatic aggression used to be based on the west coast of the American continent. The Pacific was looked upon as the avenue of possible enemy approach. Now the Pacific has become an Anglo-Saxon lake and our line of defense runs through the chain of islands fringing the coast of Asia. It starts from the Philippines and continues through the Ryukyu Archipelago, which includes the main bastion, Okinawa. Then it bends back through Japan and the Aleutian Island chain to Alaska.

Eastern policy repulsive and occasionally mentioned the General as the charismatic leader who might end the obnoxious Democratic hold on the White House. When this group transferred its attention, as Chiang did his residence, to Formosa, Senator H. Alexander Smith hinted that General MacArthur had revised upward his estimate of Formosa's military importance, a view confirmed by the memorandum that General Bradley had brought from MacArthur and read to the first Blair House meeting. A curious disclosure, earlier in the year, from the General's headquarters of a classified paper prepared for the guidance of public-affairs and press officers, which was intended to minimize the significance and damage that would result from the quite possible fall of Formosa to the Chinese Communists, suggested more than clumsy blundering, since it was received with delighted unbelief and righteous indignation by such China-bloc Senators as Knowland and Alexander Smith. And, finally, General MacArthur's eagerness to explain in person to the Generalissimo why his troop offer was not accepted should have, but did not, put us on our guard.

At the end of July the Joint Chiefs, interpreting President Truman's order not to permit an attack on or from Formosa as a change in view regarding its strategic importance (which was not the idea at all), recommended a military survey team to report on the state of its defenses.

Strange as it may seem in the light of these facts, official Washington was startled to read in the press on August 1 that General MacArthur had arrived in Formosa, kissed Mme. Chiang's hand, and gone into conference with her husband. To find out what was going on, I cabled William Sebald, Political Adviser in Tokyo, who had been appointed by the State Department. President Truman's comments evoked the admiration and envy of us all. General MacArthur's were, "To my astonishment, the visit to Formosa and my meeting with Chiang Kai-shek was greeted by a furor." [7] The Generalissimo crowed happily from Formosa that "now that we can again work closely together with our old comrade in arms" victory was assured. MacArthur reciprocated with praise of Chiang and assurances of the "effective military coordination between the Chinese and American Forces." He ordered three squadrons of jet fighters to Formosa without the knowledge of the Pentagon. Explicit orders then went to him emphasizing the limits of our policy

7. For sources of quotations of General MacArthur in this paragraph, see Douglas MacArthur, *Reminiscences* (New York: McGraw-Hill, 1964), p. 340, and Courtney Whitney, *MacArthur: His Rendezvous with Destiny* (New York: Alfred A. Knopf, 1956), pp. 372–73; for quotation of Chiang Kai-shek, see *The New York Times*, August 2, 1950.

regarding Formosa, and Harriman followed to reinforce them. A week later, on August 10, the General issued a statement that his Formosa trip had been "formally arranged and coordinated beforehand with all branches of the American and Chinese Governments." "This visit," he concluded, "has been maliciously misrepresented to the public by those who invariably in the past have propagandized a policy of defeatism and appeasement in the Pacific."

Harriman returned with an ambivalent report. On the one hand, he told the President and me that MacArthur, while disagreeing with our China and Formosa policy, had said that he was a good soldier and knew how to obey orders. Yet doubts persisted in Harriman's mind that he and MacArthur had come "to a full agreement on the way we believed things should be handled on Formosa and with the Generalissimo." [8] They certainly had not.

During the evening of August 25, Michael McDermott, Department Press Assistant, called me at Sandy Spring and read an Associated Press ticker report of a message that MacArthur had sent to the annual convention of the Veterans of Foreign Wars. Although the dispatch had gone out to member newspapers, the publication date was to be two days later. The message consisted of a long description of the strategic importance of Formosa to the United States, including the following:

Formosa in the hands of such a hostile power could be compared to an unsinkable aircraft carrier and submarine tender ideally located to accomplish offensive strategy and at the same time checkmate defensive or counter-offensive operations by friendly forces based on Okinawa and the Philippines. . . .

Nothing could be more fallacious than the threadbare argument by those who advocate appeasement and defeatism in the Pacific that if we defend Formosa we alienate continental Asia. Those who speak thus do not understand the Orient. They do not grant that it is in the pattern of Oriental psychology to respect and follow aggressive, resolute and dynamic leadership—to quickly turn on a leadership characterized by timidity or vacillation—and they underestimate the Oriental mentality.[9]

Saying that I would come to the Department early the next morning, I asked to have Rusk, Jessup, Matthews, Webb, and Harriman meet me there. All of us were outraged at the effrontery and damaging effect at home and abroad of MacArthur's message.

---

8. Truman, *Years of Trial and Hope*, p. 351.
9. Senate Committees on Armed Services and Foreign Relations, 82nd Congress, 1st Session, *Hearings to Conduct an Inquiry into the Military Situation in the Far East and the Facts Surrounding the Relief of General of the Army Douglas MacArthur from His Assignments in That Area* (hereinafter cited as *Hearings on the Military Situation in the Far East*), pp. 3479–80.

On July 19 the President had stressed to Congress and only the day before Ambassador Austin had restated to Trygve Lie, Secretary General of the United Nations, the limited purposes of our action regarding Formosa. General MacArthur had on July 8 been designated as United Nations Commander in Korea. We agreed that this insubordination could not be tolerated. MacArthur had to be forced publicly to retract his statement. Averell took the ticker dispatch to the White House.

For some time the President had had a meeting scheduled with the Secretaries of State, Treasury, and Defense, Harriman, and the Joint Chiefs of Staff for nine-thirty on that morning. When we filed into the oval office, the President, with lips white and compressed, dispensed with the usual greetings. He read the message and then asked each person around the room whether he had had any prior intimation or knowledge of it. No one had. Louis Johnson was directed to order MacArthur from the President to withdraw the message and report that he (MacArthur) had done so. The President himself would send directly to MacArthur a copy of Ambassador Austin's letter to Trygve Lie, from which he would understand why the withdrawal order was necessary. The business for which the meeting was called was hastily dispatched.

When we left the White House, nothing could have been clearer to me than that the President had issued an order to General MacArthur to withdraw the message, but Secretary Johnson soon telephoned to say that this could cause embarrassment and that he (Johnson) thought it better to inform MacArthur that if he issued the statement "we" would reply that it was "only one man's opinion and not the official policy of the Government." I said that the issue seemed to be who was President of the United States. Johnson then asked me an amazing question—whether "we dare send [MacArthur] a message that the President directs him to withdraw his statement?" I saw nothing else to do in view of the President's order.

At Johnson's request, I asked Averell Harriman whether he was clear that the President had issued an order. This shortly resulted in another call from Johnson saying that the President had dictated to him this message to go to MacArthur: "The President of the United States directs that you withdraw your message for National Encampment of Veterans of Foreign Wars, because various features with regard to Formosa are in conflict with the policy of the United States and its position in the United Nations." [10]

Still Johnson doubted the wisdom of sending the order and put

10. Truman, *Years of Trial and Hope*, p. 356.

forward his prior alternative. Stephen Early, his deputy, came on the telephone to support him, raised the question of General Mac-Arthur's right of free speech, and proposed that the President talk to General MacArthur. At this point I excused myself and ended the conversation, duly reporting it to Harriman, saying that if Johnson wished to reopen the President's decision, he should apply to the President to do so. The President instructed Harriman that he had dictated what he wanted to go and he wanted it to go. It went. MacArthur's message was both withdrawn and unofficially published.

The President has written that at this time he considered relieving General MacArthur of the Korean command while leaving him with the responsibility in Japan, but decided against it. He has been quoted later as regretting that he did not then relieve him altogether. To do so did not occur to me at the time as appropriate to the offense, although if the future had been revealed, I should have advised it even at considerable cost. General MacArthur's weakness was his incredible arrogance and vanity, which led him to surround himself with sycophants, even though some able ones. General Marshall told me of a conference he had with General MacArthur during the Second World War at which the latter began a sentence with the phrase, "My staff tells me . . ." General Marshall interrupted him, saying, "General, you don't have a staff; you have a court."

From Retreat to Counteroffensive

As American military power poured into Pusan, the long retreat down the peninsula halted and a tenuous stability was established by the Eighth Army within the Pusan perimeter. By July 20 General MacArthur, always optimistic, could cable the President that the enemy "has had his great chance and failed to exploit it." It took some weeks more of stubborn defensive fighting before we in Washington could be as convinced of this as the commanding general appeared to be, and it was not until September that our forces seized the offensive.

On September 15 the First Marine Division began its landing at Inchon on the west coast of Korea about thirty-five miles south of the 38th parallel, and approximately the same distance west of Seoul, the occupied capital of South Korea. By September 27 Seoul was recaptured and pretty well shattered in the process. General Walton Walker's Eighth Army, attacking simultaneously in the south, broke out of the Pusan perimeter and drove the retreating

North Koreans before. them until, intercepted by MacArthur's forces west of Seoul, their army was utterly destroyed by the two American forces. Perhaps thirty thousand stragglers out of an army of approximately four hundred thousand men made their escape without equipment across the parallel. By the end of the month General MacArthur's command approached the parallel, virtually without opposition.

David Rees has perceptively and with reason entitled the official Army history of the landing "Perilous Gamble or Exemplary Boldness?" [11] The Inchon counteroffensive succeeded brilliantly. It would be regarded today as one of the classic military victories of history had it not been the prelude to the greatest defeat suffered by American arms since the Battle of Manassas and an international disaster of the first water. To understand why this is so, it is necessary to look further into the nature of the Inchon operation. In doing so it would be untrue and unfair to intimate that General MacArthur should be charged with sole responsibility for disaster in Korea, though he certainly must bear the lion's share. Other mistakes were made, as will appear, to which I made a contribution.

Until August 23, General MacArthur was almost alone in favoring the risky Inchon operation. This was no mere outflanking operation but a strike deep in the enemy's rear to cut his line of communications and destroy him between the two jaws of a massive pincers. The Joint Chiefs of Staff opposed it, especially the Army and Navy chiefs, who were present in Tokyo; so did the Army, Navy, and Marine commanders who would have to carry it out. So did General Walker, commanding the Eighth Army at Pusan, for his force was to be weakened to augment the northern landing corps. If anything went wrong at Inchon, he saw himself overwhelmed by the North Koreans. And a lot could go wrong. General MacArthur himself assessed Inchon as a 5,000–to–1 risk, and saw in the very improbability of its being attempted a guarantee of an essential element in success—surprise.

The approach to Inchon harbor was narrow and rendered hazardous by rocks, shoals, and enormous tides, from an average of twenty-three to a maximum of thirty-three feet. Only a maximum tide would float the landing craft to the sea wall, which even then rose fourteen feet above the water. Maximum tides could be expected only on September 15 and October 11. At ebb tide the harbor became a mud flat, where stranded landing craft could be pounded to pieces by artillery. One does not wonder at the remark

11. David Rees, *Korea: The Limited War* (New York: St. Martin's Press, 1964), p. 95.

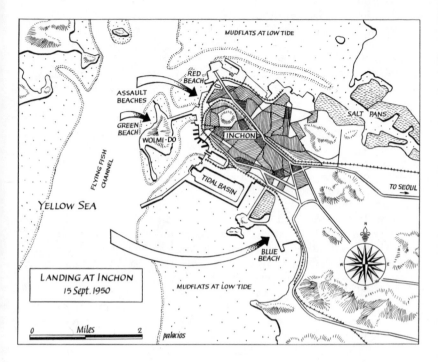

RED BEACH

ASSAULT BEACHES

GREEN BEACH

WOLMI-DO

INCHON

SALT PANS

MUDFLATS AT LOW TIDE

FLYING FISH CHANNEL

YELLOW SEA

TIDAL BASIN

TO SEOUL

BLUE BEACH

LANDING AT INCHON
15 Sept. 1950

MUDFLATS AT LOW TIDE

0   Miles   2

palacios

of a naval staff officer that they had drawn up a list of every con-
ceivable natural handicap and Inchon had them all. They were all
stated at the meeting on August 23 in General MacArthur's Tokyo
headquarters, but he brushed them aside in a brilliant defense of
his plan, ending in a dramatic hush, "I can almost hear the ticking
of the second hand of destiny. . . . We shall land at Inchon and
I shall crush them." [12]

Such was the prestige of General MacArthur—"I wish I had
that man's confidence," as Admiral Forrest Sherman put it—that
ultimately and reluctantly the Joint Chiefs of Staff and the President concurred in the Inchon operation. MacArthur's tide of luck
was in, and taken at flood led on to success. So great was his luck
that Typhoon "Kezia" with winds of a hundred and twenty-five
miles an hour, heading for the invasion fleet, veered off to the east,
and Communist spies, who had learned of the plan due to faulty
security, were unable to get word through to the North Koreans.

12. For a splendid account of the Inchon planning, landing, and a marshaling of
the authorities, see Chapter 5 of Rees, *Korea: The Limited War;* the quotation from
General MacArthur appears on p. 83.

The nickname of Inchon in Japan was "Operation Common Knowledge."

One must understand the tremendous risks assumed by General MacArthur at Inchon, and the equally great luck that saw him through, to understand the hubris that led him to assume even more impossible chances in his march to the Yalu at a time when his luck—and, unhappily, the luck of the United States also—ran out.

Conflict over a Boundary

During the summer, an opportunity had arisen to escape from Washington for a few days to be with our daughter, whom I had not seen for nearly a year. We had taken a camp at Upper St. Regis Lake, near Saranac. Thither I flew for a happy week, keeping in sketchy touch with the Department through some complicated electronic devices the Navy had supplied. Fortunately, they never worked as well for me as they were supposed to. As a result I was only peripherally involved in the dispute between State and Defense over our bombing of Rashin, a prototype of similar disputes arising over the bombing in North Vietnam seventeen years later.

Situated seventeen miles from the Soviet border with northeastern Korea, Rashin was held to have military importance because of a chemical plant and railway switching yards, in which Soviet-furnished military supplies for North Korea were said to be marshaled. On August 12, the day after I left, the Department learned that Rashin had been bombed in bad weather, with undetermined results. State protested that this bombing violated the President's orders directing U.S. military aircraft "to stay well clear" of the border, and demanded prior consultation on further sorties of this dubious nature. Secretary Johnson denied that the border had been violated, which was not the point, and refused prior consultation. On my return, I let the issue drop, but in all future cases the President himself brought us into consultation.

Coming back full of Adirondack air and happy memories, I found the Department humming with discussion of policies for both sides of the world. Events in Korea had broken inertia of thought on many critical matters—a peace treaty with Japan, German participation in her own and European defense, and what to do in Korea when the aggression had been thrown back. All were pressing for and receiving simultaneous attention. At that time the Government could and did deal with more than one crisis at a time.

In the Department two views were then locked in what seemed to me wholly unnecessary conflict. One was that under no circumstances should General MacArthur's forces cross the 38th parallel. The other denied this and advocated (or some proponents did) going wherever necessary to destroy the invader's force and restore security in the area. The latter view seemed the right one if properly restricted. Troops could not be expected, as I put it, to march up to a surveyor's line and stop. Until the actual military situation developed further, no one could say where the necessity for flexibility in tactics ended and embarkation upon a new strategic purpose began. One conclusion was clear: no arbitrary prohibition against crossing the parallel should be imposed. As a boundary it had no political validity. The next important conclusion was not clear. After knocking out the invasion and as much of the invasion force as seemed practical, what then? The official United Nations purpose was to create a unified, independent, and democratic Korea. But how and by whom? These were words and empty words; they were not policy. One of the greatest problems lay in ever getting beyond them.

In a memorandum awaiting my return, George Kennan, who was lecturing at the National War College, left me his advice on this and some other problems, a memorandum typical of its gifted author, beautifully expressed, sometimes contradictory, in which were mingled flashes of prophetic insight and suggestions, as the document itself conceded, of total impracticality. Our action in Korea, it said, was right, the aggression must be defeated and discredited, but disturbing emotional and moralistic conclusions were being drawn from this fact. It was not essential to us or within our capabilities to establish an anti-Soviet regime in all of Korea.

The Koreans could not maintain their independence against both Russian and Japanese pressures, Kennan maintained, and while Japanese influence might be preferable from our point of view to Russian, the power to exert it did not now exist. Hence it would be unrealistic to exclude the possibility of a period of Russian domination. Curiously, the memorandum did not mention what within a few months was to be a far more likely possibility—Chinese domination. Such was national interest in the abstract. In view of public opinion and political pressures in the concrete, ideas such as these could only be kept in mind as warnings not to be drawn into quicksands.

All this was good, even if purely negative, advice. It was well to be cautious. If we had been able to peer into General MacArthur's mind, we should have been infinitely more cautious than we were a few weeks later in giving him instructions and in formulating policy at the United Nations.

Uniting for Peace

On July 29 the Soviet Foreign Office had announced the end of the long, helpful Russian boycott of the United Nations Security Council. Its representative, Jacob Malik, would return to preside over it during August. His performance there following his return exceeded even lively expectations. Hickerson's bureau in the Department was put to work on the obvious problem of how to provide United Nations guidance for policy after the attack had been repelled. To repel it was the first goal set by the resolution of June 27, and it had been achieved by the end of September. The second goal was to "restore international peace and security in the area." The words were not pregnant with significance in themselves. They had been taken from Article 42 of the United Nations Charter, which empowered the Security Council, if it found "the existence of . . . any breach of the peace or act of aggression"—as it had here—to "take such action by air, sea, or land forces as may be necessary to maintain or restore international peace and security." A sensible interpretation of the resolution would have been that after repelling the armed attack the Security Council wanted to make reasonably sure that it would not be renewed as soon as the guardians of peace withdrew. Malik, wielding the Soviet veto in the Security Council, would obviously prevent the adoption there of any plan to assure peace unpalatable to the North Koreans.

However, in the light of history, the second clause in the resolution might be construed to mean something more than the prevention of a new attack. It might include a goal of the UN resolution of 1947, an independent, united Korean government, then thought a foundation, if not a prerequisite, to peace and security in the area. Behind the slogan lay a reality. The division of Korea at the 38th parallel, with the northern half in the Soviet sphere of influence and the southern half in the American, was, indeed, the chief obstacle to peace and security in the area. On the other hand, the American Government was not willing to commit its forces to the task of creating an independent and united Korea against any and all opposition.

When the Russian-created People's Republic of North Korea attacked the South and in the process lost most of its military force, the tempting possibility of achieving an independent and united Korea without more military effort or risk beckoned the United Nations. But to make this effort, or even the more modest one of preventing renewal of the attack, required a UN decision that could not be blocked by a Soviet veto in the Security Council. The purpose of my "Uniting for Peace" speech on September 20 was to make further UN decisions possible by action in the General Assembly. Some time earlier we had asked the British Foreign Office its views on a proposal to turn to the General Assembly in cases of aggression should the Security Council be paralyzed by a veto. The response was a cool one. The Foreign Office wisely forecast the dangers of the idea in the future if the then majority in the United Nations should give way to one holding contrary views. But present difficulties outweighed possible future ones, and we pressed on.

My speech [13] proposed strengthening the system of collective security within the existing Charter. It pointed out that Article 1 of the Charter ascribed to the United Nations as a whole and to its members the purpose of maintaining peace and opposing aggression. The Security Council was the principal instrument for carrying out this purpose, but if it should be paralyzed by a veto the duty remained and powers given by Articles 10, 11, and 14 gave the General Assembly responsibility and authority in maintaining international peace. We would offer a plan to increase Assembly effectiveness by: (1) providing for an emergency session of the General Assembly upon twenty-four hours' notice if the Security Council should be prevented from acting; (2) establishment by the Assembly of a security patrol—a peace patrol—to provide immediate and independent observation wherever international conflict might threaten; (3) designation by each member within its armed forces of United Nations units to be available continuously for United Nations service; and (4) establishment of a special committee to develop further means of collective action.

This plan, in a resolution sponsored by Canada, France, the Philippines, Turkey, the United Kingdom, the United States, and Uruguay, was adopted by the General Assembly on November 3, 1950, by a vote of 52 to 5, with India and Argentina abstaining. Its immediate purpose was to lay a foundation for a policy declaration by the General Assembly on the Korean situation. As it happened, however, the policy declaration was adopted on October 7, 1950, thus preceding the "Uniting for Peace" resolution by nearly a month.*

Within the United States Government, discussion of this vital policy question had been going on since the beginning of the attack. On June 29, before commitment of ground forces, I had said to the

13. *Department of State Bulletin,* Vol. XXIII, October 2, 1950, pp. 523–29.
* For a discussion of the policy statement, see pp. 57–58.

Newspaper Guild that our action in response to the UN resolutions was "solely to be for the purpose of restoring the Republic of Korea to its status prior to the invasion from the north and of reestablishing the peace broken by that aggression," [14] and on July 10 had written to Paul Nitze, director of the State Department's Policy Planning Staff, that in the immediate future "we have got to put in the force necessary to reoccupy to the 38th," subject to new problems that Russian or Chinese intervention would raise. In the longer run, if we should succeed in reoccupying the South, the question of garrisoning and supporting it would arise. This would be a hard task for us to take on, and yet it hardly seemed sensible to repel the attack and then abandon the country. I could not "see the end of it. In other words, as the Virginians say, we have bought a colt." Nowhere in my memorandum appears any thought of an independent and united Korea as the U.S. or UN war aim. Similarly, a series of discussions going on within the Government— between the President and the Secretary of State, within State, within Defense, and within the Central Intelligence Agency— seemed to approach the longer-run question through an even more immediate tactical problem: what to do about crossing the 38th parallel.

Long-range Policy and Crossing the Parallel

The President agreed that nothing should be said about post-aggression policy until the course of the fighting was much clearer than it was in mid-July, but on the seventeenth he asked the National Security Council to prepare substantive recommendations for him.

The difference of opinion that developed in the Department inhibited clear-cut thinking and led to a wait-and-see attitude. The Far Eastern Division, under Dean Rusk and John Allison, strongly urged that a crossing of the 38th parallel should not be precluded. Only events could clarify whether it should be crossed, but in their view peace and stability would not exist in Korea while the country was divided. Paul Nitze's Policy Planning Staff, influenced by George Kennan's views, took the opposite position and argued that General MacArthur should be directed to announce, as UN Commander, that his troops would not cross the parallel in pursuit if the North Korean forces withdrew to the north of it. On July 13 the problem was further complicated by President Syngman Rhee's announcement that Korean forces would not stop at the parallel and the reply of a U.S. Army spokesman that U.S. forces would

14. *Ibid.*, July 10, 1950, p. 46.

stop there and would compel South Korean troops to do likewise. I hastily cabled Ambassador John Muccio to do all he could to stop such public statements and discussion, which prejudiced the position of the United States.

Then, on July 31, planners across the river in the Pentagon made proposals of a far-reaching nature. I have long noticed that military recommendations are usually premised upon the meticulous statement of assumptions that as often as not are quite contrary to the facts and yet control the conclusions. So it was here. The recommendation was that the UN Supreme Commander should be directed to cross the parallel, defeat the enemy's forces, and occupy the country, provided the following assumptions held:

1. That the United States would mobilize sufficient resources to attain the objective and strengthen its military position in all other areas of strategic importance.

2. That the Soviet Union would not intervene in Korea or elsewhere.

3. That the President would proclaim, the Congress endorse, and the United Nations adopt as our war aim a united, free, and independent Korea, and that the United States and other nations would maintain their troops in Korea under the UN Command as occupying forces as long as needed.

Not the least interesting aspect of this remarkable intellectual exercise is that, without orders and without the existence of anything approaching these assumptions, General MacArthur would later act along the lines suggested.

On September 1 the departments had agreed through the National Security Council upon a policy recommendation dealing solely with military operations to carry out the narrow interpretation of the June 27 resolution. This concluded that the resolution was sufficient to authorize military operations north as well as south of the parallel to repel the invasion and defeat the invaders and that General MacArthur should be authorized to conduct them, provided that neither the Russians nor the Communists entered the conflict or announced their intention of doing so. The President approving, the Joint Chiefs went to work on instructions for General MacArthur—a meticulous process, which sought his comments at midmonth on an analysis of the problem.

During September, through the Indian Government, we continued to seek evidence of Chinese intentions toward Korea. Earlier Chinese troop movements into Manchuria had established a means of intervention. At first, however, Ambassador K. M. Panikkar reported Chou En-lai as emphasizing China's peaceable intentions,

in which the Indian agreed. However, after Inchon, others in Peking took a different tack and early in the morning on October 3,
Chou summoned Panikkar to the ministry to inform him that if
American troops crossed the parallel China would enter the war.
Since on the same day Andrei Vishinsky was calling on the United
Nations for a cease-fire, the withdrawal of all foreign troops, and a
coalition government to rule all Korea until national elections could
take place, it was obvious that a combined Sino-Soviet effort was
being made to save the North Korean regime. Chou's words were
a warning, not to be disregarded, but, on the other hand, not an
authoritative statement of policy.

Instructions to General MacArthur

The Joint Chiefs' instructions to General MacArthur for operations north of the 38th parallel, completed toward the end of September, approved by the State Department, and authorized by the
President, were dispatched to him on the twenty-seventh. They
contained an instruction: "You will also submit your plan for future
operations north of the 38th parallel to the JCS for approval."
General MacArthur, while protesting this order by which the Chiefs
sought to retain final approval of operations, nevertheless filed a
plan of operations on the twenty-eighth.

During these days I was in New York, presenting both our
"Uniting for Peace" proposal to the General Assembly and our
"one package" plan to the North Atlantic ministers.[15] On September 28 the President called me to Washington to discuss the developing Korean situation with him and General Marshall.[16] After
lunch in Blair House on the twenty-ninth an officer, with the aid
of a large map of Korea showing the position of all American, South
Korean, and North Korean units, described the movements proposed by General MacArthur.

First, the Joint Chiefs of Staff instructions of September 27:

15. The "one-package plan" is discussed in *Present at the Creation,* Chapters
46–49. The purpose was to solve the basic problem of the defense of Europe. It was
agreed in the U.S. Government that the defense needed strengthening, which would
have to be provided by increased allied forces, increased American troops and military
aid, and the inclusion of armed German units; and that all this would have to be inte-
grated and directed by a united command. Although the Defense Department
foresaw the trouble inclusion of German units would cause with the United Kingdom
and France, it insisted that all of this must be obtained in "one package," whereas it
seemed to me wiser to establish the united command, leaving it to the logic of mathe-
matics to convince everyone that no plan would be tenable without Germany.

16. On September 12, the President had announced that General George C.
Marshall would replace Louis Johnson as Secretary of Defense. Shortly thereafter
Robert A. Lovett was named Deputy Secretary of Defense. A year later he succeeded
General Marshall as Secretary of Defense.

Your military objective is the destruction of the North Korean Armed Forces. In attaining this objective you are authorized to conduct military operations, including amphibious and airborne landings or ground operations north of the 38th parallel in Korea, provided that at the time of such operations there has been no entry into North Korea by major Soviet or Chinese Communist Forces, no announcement of intended entry, nor a threat to counter our operations militarily in North Korea. Under no circumstances, however, will your forces cross the Manchurian or USSR borders of Korea and, as a matter of policy, no non-Korean Ground Forces will be used in the northeast provinces bordering the Soviet Union or in the area along the Manchurian border. Furthermore support of your operations north or south of the 38th parallel will not include Air or Naval action against Manchuria or against USSR territory.

In the event of the open or covert employment of major Soviet units south of the 38th parallel, you will assume the defense, make no move to aggravate the situation and report to Washington. You should take the same action in the event your forces are operating north of the 38th parallel, and major Soviet units are openly employed. You will not discontinue Air and Naval operations north of the 38th parallel merely because the presence of Soviet or Chinese Communist troops is detected in a target area, but if the Soviet Union or Chinese Communists should announce in advance their intention to reoccupy North Korea and give warning, either explicitly or implicitly, that their forces should not be attacked you should refer the matter to Washington.[17]

The General proposed to send the Eighth Army across the parallel on the west coast through Kaesong and Sariwon to take the northern capital, Pyongyang, while the X Corps would be water-lifted to Wonsan on the east coast. It would link up with the western troops along the Wonsan-Pyongyang road. (Unfortunately, mine-clearing in Wonsan harbor delayed the landing until October 26, enabling the North Korean Army to escape through the gap. Korean troops sent overland arrived at Wonsan on October 11.) Mindful of the warning in the directive, the General proposed to use only South Korean troops north of the line Chungjo-Yongwon-Hungnam, about fifty miles north of Pyongyang-Wonsan and sixty miles southeast of the Yalu at its mouth. He would provide detailed plans later and ended by saying that there was no indication of "present entry into North Korea by major Soviet or Chinese communist forces."

The plan seemed excellently contrived to create a strong military position from which to exploit the possibilities of the North Korean defeat—either to insure the South by a strong defensive line against a renewal of the attack or, if the South Koreans were strong enough and the Chinese did not intervene, to move toward the UN goal of a united, independent, and democratic Korea. With these thoughts in mind General Marshall and I recommended, and the President approved, the plan of operation.

The same day General Marshall sent General MacArthur a for his "eyes only" telegram saying, "We want you to feel unhampered tactically and strategically to proceed north of the 38th parallel," to which MacArthur replied, "Unless and until the enemy capitulates, I regard all Korea as open for our military operations." Later this exchange was to cause trouble, MacArthur citing it along with other implausible evidence as release from the inhibition against using other than Korean troops in the northern-border provinces. Although I had no knowledge of the messages at the time, it is inconceivable that General Marshall should have arrogated to himself authority to give General MacArthur dispensation to violate instructions from the Joint Chiefs of Staff approved by the President and MacArthur's own plan of operations also approved by the President and himself that very day. To me, the message seems directed toward soothing MacArthur's irritation at being required to submit his plan of operations. He was assured that Washington wanted him to feel unhampered in proceeding north, except as his orders confined him. His plan showed that he understood this perfectly.

"A Unified, Independent and Democratic Korea"

A resolution * to restate UN policy for Korea had been drafted with our participation and on September 30 was introduced by Kenneth Younger, co-sponsored by Australia, Brazil, Cuba, the Netherlands, Norway, Pakistan, and the Philippines. It represented a view that had been growing in the Far Eastern and United Nations divisions of the Department during August and was given a strong push by the success at Inchon. Ambassador Ernest Gross had discussed the idea during August with India's Sir Benegal Rau, and Ambassador Austin put up a trial balloon by a speech in the Security Council on August 17. Both seemed to win a favorable reception. The trouble inherent in the resolution itself and in the encouragement it gave to General MacArthur's adventurism lay in the fact that it was not thought through and it masked in ambivalent language the difficulties and dangers against which Kennan had warned in the memorandum discussed earlier.

* See page 52.

In effect, the resolution revived the dormant United Nations plan of 1947 for what it called "a unified, independent and democratic government" of Korea. This long-term aim was to be achieved by (1) insuring conditions of stability throughout the country, (2) holding elections under UN auspices and taking other constituent acts necessary to establish the government, (3) inviting all sections and representative bodies in the country to cooperate with the United Nations in this effort, (4) maintaining UN forces in the country only as long as necessary to achieve these objectives, and (5) providing for the economic rehabilitation of Korea. The resolution was passed October 7.

Behind this proposal lay the belief that effort to carry out the 1947 resolution had been blocked by Soviet military power. Soviet forces, however, had been withdrawn and the substituted North Korean troops defeated and scattered. No opposing military force remained in the north to frustrate UN efforts, and the chances were believed good that neither Russian nor Chinese troops would intervene if only Korean soldiery attempted to establish whatever degree of order was possible in the rugged country of the extreme north, where even the Japanese had had only nominal sovereignty. If the Koreans encountered too heavy resistance, they could fall back to the strong position across the neck. In the light of retrospect, this seems a naïve view of the probabilities, but retrospect is to some degree colored by MacArthur's subsequent conduct. If, for instance, General Matthew B. Ridgway had been given the task of carrying out the instructions of September 27–29 and such orders as would have come to him from Washington to assist the UN Commission in charge of operations under the October 7 resolution, the results would most certainly have been different. With the cast of characters as it was, however, the resolution of October 7 increased the hazards, for which I must bear a measure of responsibility.

General MacArthur at once stripped from the resolution of October 7 its husk of ambivalence and gave it an interpretation that the enacting majority in the General Assembly would not have accepted. Nowhere did the resolution declare that the Eighth Army would impose a unified and democratic government on all Korea. Its task was to "ensure conditions of stability throughout Korea." On October 9 General MacArthur broadcast a second surrender demand, quoting the resolution of the seventh and declaring: "In order that the decisions of the United Nations may be carried out . . . I . . . for the last time, call upon you and the forces under your command . . . forthwith to lay down your arms and cease hostilities. . . . Unless immediate response is made by you . . . I shall at once proceed to take such military action as may be necessary to enforce the decrees of the United Nations." [18] If there had been doubt before that "the unified, independent and democratic government of Korea" would, so far as the Supreme Commander was concerned, be established by his "terrible, swift sword," it was now removed.

Early in October President Truman conceived the idea of meeting General MacArthur on Wake Island in the mid-Pacific for a heart-to-heart talk that would establish a thorough understanding between them. Each man was to think that an understanding had been established, but each would have a different idea of what it was.

18. *Hearings on the Military Situation in the Far East*, p. 3483.

III

LOST CHANCES

Pilgrimage to Wake

WHEN THE PRESIDENT told me of his intended pilgrimage to Wake Island and invited me to join him, I begged to be excused. While General MacArthur had many of the attributes of a foreign sovereign, I said, and was quite as difficult as any, it did not seem wise to recognize him as one. It was agreed between us that what the President might need from the State Department could be furnished by Ambassador John Muccio, Dean Rusk, Philip Jessup, and Averell Harriman, all of whom would be there. I had not been consulted in arriving at the decision to hold the meeting and offered no suggestions after it had been made. The whole idea was distasteful to me. I wanted no part in it, and saw no good coming from it. I could not then or now explain this strong presentiment, beyond the conviction that talk should precede, not follow, the issuance of orders. The latter only befogs them. So I contented myself with seeing the President off on October 11 and welcoming him back on the eighteenth.

The President and General MacArthur spent between two and a half and three hours together, from approximately six-thirty in the morning to a little after nine. For half of that time they were alone. The President has written his recollection of the talk.[1] We were soon to get an intimation of the General's; it bore out my worst forebodings. The discussion that followed with colleagues present was more immediately and fully reported—more fully, due to a circumstance that was later to cause the proverbial tempest in a teapot. Miss Vernice Anderson, Ambassador Jessup's secretary,

---

1. Truman, *Years of Trial and Hope*, pp. 365–70.

During his visit to Wake Island, President Truman awards the Distinguished Service Medal to General MacArthur, as John Muccio, U. S. Ambassador to South Korea, looks on. WARDER COLLECTION

October 18, 1950. General Marshall, at that time Secretary of Defense, and the author greet the President on his return from a deceptively congenial meeting with General MacArthur on Wake Island. ACME

was waiting next door to the conference room to help with the communiqué. The door was open and the conversation audible. Having nothing to do and knowing that a memorandum of conversation would be worked out on the way home, she took stenographic notes. When this became known at the hearings on General Mac-Arthur's relief, charges were made that it was akin to "bugging" the conference. This was utter nonsense.

In the large meeting the General expressed optimistic views that the end of the fighting was close (he had told the President probably by Thanksgiving and that our troops, except for two divisions, could begin withdrawal from Korea by Christmas) and that the Chinese would not intervene. If, however, they should do so, not more than fifty to sixty thousand could cross the Yalu, and they would be slaughtered if they attempted to go south. The party returned full of optimism and confidence in the General. The President's speech two days later in the San Francisco Opera House exuded both. In explaining his journey to Wake, he concluded: "I also felt that there was pressing need to make it perfectly clear— by my talk with General MacArthur—that there is complete unity in the aims and conduct of our foreign policy." That perfect clarity did not outlast the month.

MacArthur Moves North

By mid-October General MacArthur's forces had reached the line established in accordance with his plan of operations approved September 29. North of this line the plan permitted the use of Korean troops only.

On the twenty-fourth General MacArthur without warning or notice to Washington ordered his commanders to "drive forward with all speed and full utilization of their forces." [2] The restraining line in the north was thus abolished and with it the inhibition against other than South Korean troops in the border provinces. The Army moved swiftly. One element of the Eighth Army, the 7th Regiment of the South Korean 6th Division, reached the Yalu near Chosan on October 26 without opposition and turned back. Then things began to happen. So stunned was the Pentagon that the Joint Chiefs of Staff sent out a timorous inquiry to MacArthur

2. The message of October 24, RAD CX 67291, CINCUNC to All Commanders 24 Oct. 50, and the JCS inquiry, RAD JCS 94933, JCS Personal to MacArthur, 24 Oct. 50, all seen in Schnabel, *Policy and Direction*. General MacArthur's reply to JCS inquiry has been put together from texts in *Hearings on the Military Situation in the Far East*, p. 1241; Truman, *Years of Trial and Hope*, p. 372; and Schnabel, *Policy and Direction*.

saying that although he undoubtedly had sound reasons for issuing this order they would like to be informed of them "as your action is a matter of some concern here," a magnificent understatement. Back came one of the purple telegrams with which we were to become familiar during November as the drive north ran its ill-fated course. General MacArthur had lifted the restriction "as a matter of military necessity," since the South Korean troops were neither sufficiently strong nor well-enough led to handle the situation. (In which case, it had been supposed that they would be withdrawn to the supporting line.) The directive of September 27 was not, he said, a "final directive," since it stated that it might later be amended (a proposition true also of the Constitution of the United States). Furthermore, he said, the Chiefs of Staff had not banned the use of other than South Korean forces in the extreme north, but had merely stated that "it should not be done as a matter of policy." In any event, he continued, General Marshall's cable of September 29 had modified prior instruction of the Chiefs. General MacArthur understood "the basic purpose and intent of your directive, and every possible precaution is being taken in the premises. The very reverse, however, would be fostered and tactical hazards might even result from other action than that which I have directed." Then the final clincher: "This entire subject was covered in my conference at Wake Island." President Truman stated on October 26 that it was his understanding that only Korean troops would approach the northern border. However, General MacArthur replied through the press on the twenty-seventh that "the mission of the UN force is to clear Korea."

"Tactical hazards" immediately encountered were somewhat different in nature from those of which the General had warned. On October 26 the 7th Regiment of the South Korean 6th Division, returning as reported from the Yalu, blundered into a large concentration of Chinese troops, which had already crossed the river, and was destroyed. The next day the South Korean II Corps to the north of Unsan in northwest Korea and the 5th and 8th U.S. Cavalry to the west of it were attacked by overwhelming force. At the end of four days and nights of incessant and often hand-to-hand fighting the II Corps was no longer an organized force and the 8th Cavalry had lost half its strength and most of its equipment. The enemy broke contact and General Walton Walker regrouped II Corps back at the Chongchon River, reporting to General MacArthur that he had been ambushed by "well organized and well trained units."

Schizophrenia at GHQ

It took time for report of the events of October 25–November 1 to percolate from North Korea through Tokyo to Washington, if, indeed, it ever did percolate in recognizable form. For instance, in a press conference on November 1,[3] I reported that the UN Command was investigating the reported presence of Chinese Communist troops in Korea. The survivors of the 8th Cavalry regiment might have thought the fact established. Meanwhile Russian MIG-15 jets made their first appearance over Korea on October 31. MacArthur's reports were schizophrenic. On November 4, responding to the President's request for fuller information, he sent a calming evaluation warning against "hasty conclusions which might be premature" and urging patience during "a more complete accumulation of military facts." [4]

However, within twenty-four hours he was rejecting his own advice. By October 25, the restrictions on the U.S. Fifth Air Force had been eased to allow close support missions "under control of a tactical air control party or a Mosquito observer, as near the border as necessary." However, there was to be no bombing within five miles of the border. In spite of all instructions on October 9, U.S. planes as the result of acknowledged "navigation error and bad judgment" had fired on an airfield a hundred kilometers inside Soviet territory, for which we expressed regret and offered to pay damages. Now, on November 5, General MacArthur ordered General George E. Stratemeyer to use his full air power to knock the North Koreans and their allies out of the war.[5] "Combat crews are to be flown to exhaustion if necessary," the Korean ends of all Yalu bridges were to be taken out, and, excepting Rashin, Suiho Dam, and other hydroelectric plants, every means of communication, installation, factory, city and village in North Korea, destroyed. He also informed the UN Security Council that the UN forces "are presently in hostile contact with Chinese Communist military units," listing twelve encounters.[6]

General Stratemeyer informed the Pentagon of his orders three hours before his planes were due to take off on their mission against the bridges from Sinuiju to Antung. Shortly after ten o'clock that

3. *The New York Times,* November 2, 1950.
4. Truman, *Years of Trial and Hope,* p. 373, and RAD C68285, CINCFE to DA for CSUSA for JCS, 4 Nov. 50, as seen in Schnabel, *Policy and Direction.*
5. USAF Historical Study No. 72, *United States Air Force Operations in the Korean Conflict, 1 Nov. 1950–30 June 1953* (Washington, D.C.: Air Force, Historical Division, 1955 and 1956), p. 22.
6. *Department of State Bulletin,* Vol. XXIII, November 27, 1950, p. 858.

morning Deputy Secretary of Defense Robert Lovett brought the order to me in the State Department, saying that he doubted whether the bombing would importantly interrupt traffic across the river and that the danger of bombing the Manchurian city of An-tung was great. Mr. Rusk, who was with us, contributed that we were committed not to attack Manchurian points without consul-tation with the British and that their Cabinet was meeting that morning to reconsider their attitude toward the Chinese Communist Government. We had also asked the UN Security Council for an urgent meeting to consider General MacArthur's report of Chinese intervention in Korea. Ill-considered action at this moment could be unfortunate. We agreed and telephoned General Marshall, who thought that the Joint Chiefs of Staff should be asked to postpone MacArthur's action until the President's instructions could be ob-tained. This was done.

Fortunately, the President was reached by telephone in Kansas City on his way home to vote. I explained the situation, adding that MacArthur's reports as late as the day before had contained no hint of movements across the river. The President said that he would authorize anything necessary for the security of the troops. Could I, he asked, call MacArthur and ascertain the facts? I replied, and he agreed, that communications with MacArthur on military matters should be through military channels. The President told me to handle the matter as Lovett and I thought best, adding that he would be available by telephone if needed and that the security of the troops should not be jeopardized. Subject to that, he agreed on the importance of postponing the action until we had a statement of the justifying facts.

Lovett left with a summary of the President's views for the meeting of the Joint Chiefs at eleven-fifteen that morning, just one and three-quarters hours before Stratemeyer's planes were due to take off unless already stopped. The Chiefs reaffirmed their order against bombing within five miles of the border, stated that the Government was committed not to take action affecting Manchuria without consulting the British, and asked for MacArthur's reasons for bombing the bridges. Back came another purple paragraph:

Men and material in large force are pouring across all bridges over the Yalu from Manchuria. This movement not only jeopardizes but threatens the ultimate destruction of the forces under my command. . . . The only way to stop this reinforcement of the enemy is the destruction of these bridges and the subjection of all installations in the north area supporting the enemy advance to the maximum of our air destruction. . . . Under the gravest protest that I can make, I am suspending this strike [at Sinuiju] and carrying out your instructions. . . . I trust that the matter be immediately brought to the attention of the President as I believe your instructions may well result in a calamity of major proportion.[7]

Since MacArthur was in responsible command and represented the emergency as so urgent, the President—as he expressed it— "told Bradley to give him the 'go-ahead.' " The skepticism of the Chiefs shows through the correct language of their reply:

The situation depicted in your message [of November 6] is considerably changed from that reported in last sentence your message [of November 4] which was our last report from you. We agree that the destruction of the Yalu bridges would contribute materially to the security of the forces under your command unless this action resulted in increased Chinese Communist effort and even Soviet contribution in response to what they might well construe as an attack on Manchuria.

However, in view of first sentence your message [of November 6] you are authorized to go ahead with your planned bombing in Korea near the frontier including targets at Sinuiju and Korean end of Yalu bridges provided that at time of receipt of this message you still find such action essential to safety of your forces. The above does not authorize the bombing of any dams or power plants on the Yalu River.[8]

MacArthur's messages of November 6 and 7 confused the situation for those of us in Washington even more than it had been before.

The first one, a public communiqué,[9] depicted the "practical end" of the war with the North Koreans by his capture of their capital and destruction of their army. Then had begun a wholly new war by a new enemy, the Communist Chinese, through "one of the most offensive acts of international lawlessness of historic record"— i.e., crossing the Yalu. The new enemy had also massed reinforcing divisions behind the river in a "privileged sanctuary." "A possible trap" was avoided with minimum losses only by "timely detection and skillful maneuvering"—a euphemistic phrase for running into an ambush. His mission he saw as defeating the forces arrayed against him in North Korea (presumably the new enemy) and achieving the United Nations objective of bringing unity and peace to the Korean people.

The next day, November 7, MacArthur added to his public message, with its implied criticism of the Government's policy, two private judgments.[10] In one he concluded that his estimate of

---

7. Truman, *Years of Trial and Hope*, p. 375.
8. *Ibid.*, p. 376.
9. *Department of State Bulletin*, Vol. XXIII, November 13, 1950, p. 763.
10. Truman, *Years of Trial and Hope*, p. 377, and JCS C68445, 7 Nov. 50, as seen in Schnabel, *Policy and Direction*.

November 4 that the Chinese had not made a full-scale intervention had been right, although they might be able to force on him a "movement in retrograde." However, he was planning to move forward to take "accurate measure . . . of enemy strength." The second message of November 7 contained a strong protest against the "present restrictions"—that is, against planes flying over Manchuria—which "provide a complete sanctuary for hostile air immediately upon their crossing the Manchuria-North Korean border." This was to lead to the "hot pursuit" argument, which broke out some days later. On November 9 he cabled his opinion that with his "air power, now unrestricted so far as Korea is concerned, . . . I can deny reinforcements coming across the Yalu in sufficient strength to prevent the destruction [sic] of those forces now arrayed against me in North Korea." [11]

The five days from November 4 to 9 give an excellent example of General MacArthur's mercurial temperament. In this period he went from calm confidence, warning against hasty judgment until all the facts were in, through ringing the tocsin on the sixth to proclaim that hordes of men were pouring into Korea and threatening to overwhelm his command, to confidence again on the ninth that he could deny the enemy reinforcement and destroy him. In fact, his troops were being secretly surrounded by overpowering numbers of Chinese.

Washington could not follow his moods. During the depressive period of November 6–8 the Chiefs of Staff informed him that his "objective" (the destruction of the North Korean Army) stated in the September 27 directive might have to be re-examined as the eventuality mentioned in it—the entry of Communist China into the war—seemed to have occurred. This suggestion drove MacArthur to manic reaction and deep into the realm of United Nations political policy. It would be fatal to weaken the UN policy of destroying resisting forces and bringing unity and freedom to Korea, he said. Anything less would destroy the "morale of my forces and its psychological consequences would be inestimable." To give up any portion of Korea to aggression would be immoral, bankrupt our leadership, and make our position untenable, politically and militarily. He deprecated the "Munich attitude" of the British. He meant to launch his attack about November 15 and to keep on going until he got to the border.[12]

11. CINCFE to DA for JCS C68572, 9 Nov. 50, as seen in Roy E. Appleman, *South to the Naktong, North to the Yalu* (Washington, D.C.: Department of the Army, Office of the Chief of Military History, 1956), p. 765.
12. Summary from Schnabel, *Policy and Direction,* RAD C68572, CINCFE to DA for JCS, 9 Nov. 50.

The Joint Chiefs were intimidated but not convinced by this blast. They believed, as they always had, that Chinese power, if the Chinese chose to exert it, could be defeated militarily only by a greater concentration of American military power in this area than our interests and needs in other areas warranted. The goal of a free and united Korea belonged, if it were achievable at all, in the field of diplomatic effort. Therefore, they recommended—with presidential approval through the National Security Council—that the mission assigned to General MacArthur should be kept under review but not changed at that time.

The Last Clear Chance

Here, I believe, the Government missed its last chance to halt the march to disaster in Korea. All the President's advisers in this matter, civilian and military, knew that something was badly wrong, though what it was, how to find out, and what to do about it they muffed. That they were deeply disturbed and felt the need for common counsel is shown by the unprecedented fact that in the three weeks and three days from November 10 until December 4, when disaster was full upon us, the Secretaries of State and Defense and their chief assistants met three times with the Chiefs of Staff in their war room to tussle with the problem, the two secretaries met five times with the President, and I consulted with him on five other occasions. I have an unhappy conviction that none of us, myself prominently included, served him as he was entitled to be served.

Our bafflement centered about the two principal enigmas of this situation. What were the facts about Chinese military presence in North Korea and what were Chinese intentions? (The first would throw light on the second.) And what was General MacArthur up to in the amazing military maneuver that was unfolding before unbelieving eyes? Regarding the first, the forces that had struck the Eighth Army during the last days of October and the opening days of November had been powerful, fully equipped, and competent— and yet they seemed to have vanished from the earth. The most elementary caution would seem to warn that they might, indeed probably would, reappear as suddenly and harmfully as they had before.

However, General MacArthur was taking no precautions. As at Inchon, he had divided his forces in the presence of the enemy. The Eighth Army under General Walker in the west and the X

Corps under General Edward M. Almond in the east were widely separated, leaving both their flanks exposed. Their only coordination came through Tokyo on the basis of intelligence thirty hours old when received. Moreover, division of forces had been carried further. The X Corps moved north in three separate columns through rugged country without capacity of mutual support. The Eighth Army was likewise divided into four or more separate columns covering a broad front with little or no lateral connection. Winter was coming on fast, when the frozen Yalu would furnish easy crossing without regard to bridges. Here surely was a soldier's nightmare, equally ill adapted to taking "accurate measure . . . of enemy strength" (the November 7 declared purpose) and to reaching and holding the border in the face of winter.

At our first meeting with General Marshall and the Chiefs of Staff on November 21, after General Ridgway had pointed out the startling dispositions, I stated our concerns. General MacArthur seemed to have confused his military directive (to follow and destroy the remnant of the North Korean Army unless Chinese intervention in force made it evident that he could not succeed in this task) with his civil affairs directive intended to follow military success (helping the UN Commission establish a government for a united Korea). At this point our object was not "real estate" but an army. An attempt to establish a united Korea by force of arms against a determined Chinese resistance could easily lead into general hostilities, since both the Chinese and the Russians, as well as the Japanese, had all regarded Korea as a road to somewhere else rather than an end in itself. Very definitely the policy of our Government was to avoid general war in Asia. Apparently General MacArthur could not determine the degree of Chinese intervention without some sort of a "probe" along his line; therefore we did not oppose that. When I privately expressed a layman's concern to Generals Marshall and Bradley over MacArthur's scattering of his forces, they pointed out that the Chiefs of Staff, seven thousand miles from the front, could not direct the theater commander's dispositions. But under this obvious truth lay, I felt, uneasy respect for the Mac-Arthur mystique. Strange as these maneuverings appeared, they could be another 5,000–to–1 shot by the sorcerer of Inchon. Though no one could explain them, and General MacArthur would not, no one would restrain them.

Going on to diplomatic methods of easing the dangerous showdown that might be coming by such a method as Bevin favored—a cease-fire and a demilitarized zone along the border—or as others had urged by falling back to the neck of Korea, concentrating our forces, and doing our probing with Korean forces, as was thought to be Government policy at the end of September, I was sure that General MacArthur would frustrate any such efforts until he had felt out Chinese strength. Accordingly, I had persuaded the British to hold up any initiative in the United Nations. Finally, I said that clearly no troops would be released from the Far East by Christmas, or for a long time afterward, and that, as NSC-68 had pointed out, military strength was badly needed elsewhere. Hence our establishment must be increased to provide it. From this conclusion and from the one that General MacArthur had to have his try no one dissented. The rest of the discussion went over old ground but presented no new ideas.

When we met again in the National Security Council a week later, the whole face of things had changed. On November 17 MacArthur had informed the Chiefs that on the twenty-fourth he would start a general offensive to attain the line of the Yalu.[13] His air attacks had isolated the battlefield from enemy reinforcements. While the supply situation was unsatisfactory, he nevertheless proposed to clear the country of enemy forces before the Yalu froze and furnished a crossing for overwhelming numbers. Such was the reasoning. A cautionary cable from the Chiefs of Staff urging him to stop on the high ground commanding the Yalu valley was brushed aside as "utterly impossible." In the full optimism of the manic tide he flew to Eighth Army headquarters on the Chongchon River and proclaimed the general offensive in the northwest, declaring, "If successful this should for all practical purposes end the war, restore peace and unity to Korea, enable the prompt withdrawal of United Nations military forces, and permit the complete assumption by the Korean people and nation of full sovereignty and international equality." [14]

As I look back, the critical period stands out as the three weeks from October 26 to November 17. Then all the dangers from dispersal of our own forces and intervention by the Chinese were manifest. We were all deeply apprehensive. We were frank with one another, but not quite frank enough. I was unwilling to urge on the President a military course that his military advisers would not propose.[15] They would not propose it because it ran counter to

13. MSG C69211, CINCUNC to DA, 18 Nov. 50, Schnabel, *Policy and Direction*, cited in Appleman, *South to the Naktong, North to the Yalu*, p. 774.
14. *Hearings on the Military Situation in the Far East*, p. 3492.
15. Martin Lichterman, in his study "To the Yalu and Back" in *American Civil Military Decisions*, edited by Harold Stein (Tuscaloosa: University of Alabama Press,

Secretary of Defense Marshall and the author leave the White House after the November 28 meeting of the National Security Council. ACME

American military tradition of the proper powers of the theater commander since 1864. President Lincoln had stopped meddling by Washington in military operations, had appointed Grant a lieutenant general, and had put him in full command of the armies of the United States. If General Marshall and the Chiefs had proposed withdrawal to the Pyongyang-Wonsan line and a continuous defensive position under united command across it—and if the President had backed them, as he undoubtedly would have—disaster would probably have been averted. But it would have meant a fight with MacArthur, charges by him that they had denied him victory—which they, perhaps, would have uneasily felt might have been true—and his relief under arguable circumstances. So they hesitated, wavered, and the chance was lost. While everyone acted correctly, no one, I suspect, was ever quite satisfied with himself afterward. Undoubtedly the same might have been true had we all played it the other way. It is a good bet that had we done so MacArthur's reputation would be higher today.

1963, p. 602), attributes to me a statement that goes much farther than this one. Quite incorrectly, he quotes me as telling him that Secretary Marshall and the Joint Chiefs of Staff asked me to recommend to the President that he issue an order to General MacArthur to halt his advance and consolidate his position, adding that they would not make such a recommendation themselves. He cites as authority a letter from me of January 30, 1957, and an interview of March 27, 1957. The letter contains no such statement but contains a criticism of a wholly different point in his study. I have no memorandum or recollection of the interview.

I have discussed this alleged statement of mine with General J. Lawton Collins and reaffirm what I said to him, that no such request was made to me. A footnote on this matter in Chapter 8 of General Collins' book, *War in Peacetime* (Boston: Houghton Mifflin Company, 1969), p. 202, is entirely correct.

IV

"AN ENTIRELY NEW WAR"

THE ARMY, against the deepest forebodings of General Walker, moved forward into the ominously silent and apparently deserted mountain area of northwest Korea. Four days later massive Chinese counterattacks exploded all around its many columns, in their front, on their flanks, and in their rear. A series of fiercely fought and largely separate battles developed. General MacArthur plunged from the height of optimism to the bottom of his depressive cycle. "We face an entirely new war," he reported on November 28. "This has shattered the high hopes we entertained . . . that . . . the war in Korea could be brought to a rapid close by our movement to the international boundary and the prompt withdrawal thereafter of United Nations forces." [1] All hope of localizing the Korean conflict, he cabled the Joint Chiefs of Staff, was gone. The Chinese wanted nothing less than the "complete destruction" of his army. What had been shattered was MacArthur's dream, the product of his own hubris. Unfortunately the Eighth Army was to be pretty well shattered also.

In this atmosphere the National Security Council met on the same day. General Bradley led off with a summary of the military situation so far as known. General MacArthur under heavy attack had turned to the defensive. The offensive had been to find out the dimension of Chinese intervention; now we knew. The extent of our predicament and the nature of new directives must await clarifications. The three hundred aircraft, including two hundred bombers, on Manchurian airfields constituted a serious threat to our forces and our planes crowded on Korean fields. To bomb them invited retaliation from Chinese and Russian aircraft. So far they

1. *Hearings on the Military Situation in the Far East*, p. 3495.

were quiescent. General Vandenberg concurred in not initiating the bombing, certainly not until some of our own planes had been removed to Japan.

General Marshall produced a report by three service secretaries, with which he and the Joint Chiefs agreed, recommending that we should continue to act as the executive agent of the United Nations and with its support, not be drawn into a separate conflict with Communist China. Hence we should use all means to keep the war limited, not strike Chinese territory, not use Chinese Nationalist forces (which, the Chiefs noted, might cause withdrawal of the much more effective British forces). They also urged a rapid increase in U.S. military power to meet increasing needs for it.

In Korea, Generals Marshall, Bradley, and Collins pointed out, General MacArthur would have to get along with the forces he had. Troops for replacement of losses would not be ready until the new year, nor new divisions until after March 1, 1951. Then competing demands for the latter would be heavy. All the soldiers were distressed at General MacArthur's exposed and scattered tactical position. They would call his attention to it, but it was for him to solve; it would not help to interfere with operations on the spot. Vice President Barkley, in obviously sincere puzzlement, caused some embarrassment by wondering what General MacArthur had in mind in making his statement about getting the troops out of Korea by Christmas. Could it have been a hoax for the Chinese? Unhelpfully the President said that he would have to draw his own conclusions. In General Bradley's view General MacArthur had full confidence in the success of his attack and no inkling of the strong concentration in the high mountains on his right. It certainly was no hoax. To General Marshall it was an embarrassment that we must get around in some manner.

My own views were that we were closer than we had yet been to a wider war. There had always been a Chinese involvement in Korea. It had been progressively uncloaked until now we faced a full-scale attack. Behind this was the somber possibility of Soviet support in any one of many forms. We should consider Korea not in isolation but in its worldwide setting of our confrontation with our Soviet antagonist. We had objectives to reach and dangers to avoid. The State Department would take on the task of uniting the United Nations against the Chinese Communist aggression and branding it as such, regardless of a Soviet veto in the Security Council. The memorandum of the three secretaries and the comments were very wise. General MacArthur faced a new situation. This time we should see that he understood his instructions. He

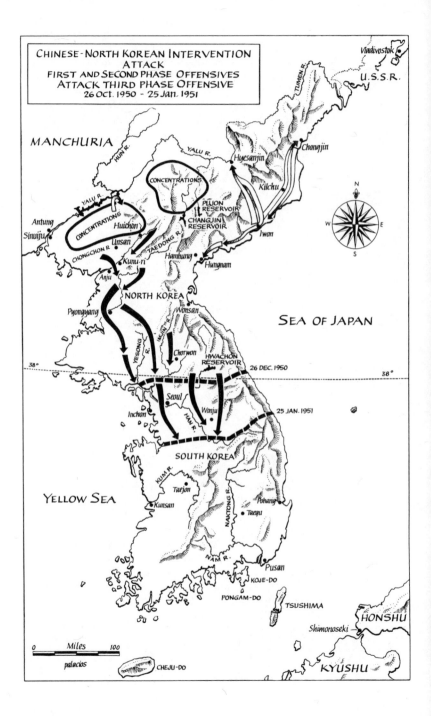

CHINESE-NORTH KOREAN INTERVENTION
ATTACK
FIRST AND SECOND PHASE OFFENSIVES
ATTACK THIRD PHASE OFFENSIVE
26 Oct. 1950 - 25 Jan. 1951

MANCHURIA

YALU R.

HUN R.

YALU R.

CONCENTRATIONS

Vladivostok

U.S.S.R.

Chongjin

Hyesanjin

Kilchu

PUJON
RESERVOIR

CHANGJIN
RESERVOIR

Iwon

Antung

Sinuiju

CONCENTRATIONS

Huichon

Unsan

CHONGCHON R.

Kunu-ri

Anju

NORTH KOREA

TAEDONG R.

Hamhung

Hungnam

Pyongyang

Wonsan

SEA OF JAPAN

YESONG R.

IMJIN R.

Chorwon

HWACHON
RESERVOIR

26 DEC. 1950

38°

38°

Inchon

Seoul

HAN R.

Wonju

25 JAN. 1951

SOUTH KOREA

KUM R.

YELLOW SEA

Taejon

Kunsan

NAKTONG R.

Pohang

Taegu

N

W   E

S

Pusan

NAM R.

KOJE-DO

PONGAM-DO

TSUSHIMA

HONSHU

Shimonoseki

0   Miles   100

palacios

CHEJU-DO

KYUSHU

seemed to have been under the misapprehension that he was supposed to occupy the north and northeastern parts of Korea. We
should tell him plainly that that was not his mission. We wanted
to terminate that involvement. We could not defeat the Chinese
in Korea because they could put in more men than we could afford
to commit there.

The imperative step was to find a line that we could hold and
hold it. Such proposals as a cease-fire or demilitarized zone in the
North could be considered, but there was no indication that any
such arrangements could be made. To pull out of Korea at this
stage would be disastrous for us. Outside of Korea we should speed
building our own military strength and that of our European allies.

The meeting ended without recommendations for decisions by
the President.

Disaster Rattles the General

The next few days were a time of anxiety and confusion as the
debacle in Korea deepened and General MacArthur's depression
grew to near panic. When, on November 29, the Chiefs of Staff
urged him to coordinate the Eighth Army and X Corps "to prevent
any enemy forces from passing between them or outflanking either
of them," he rejected the advice and called for reinforcements and
new directives.[2] On the twenty-eighth he sent a message to Ray-
Henle of the *Three-Star Extra* news broadcast explaining his position,[3] on the thirtieth, another to Arthur Krock of *The New York
Times* justifying his march north; and on December 1 gave an
interview to *U.S. News & World Report* in which he said that
orders forbidding him to strike at Communist forces across the
Manchurian border had put UN forces under "an enormous handicap, without precedent in military history." Others followed to the
United Press, International News Service, the *London Daily Mail*,
and the Tokyo press corps.

At length (December 5), his patience exhausted, the President
ordered a moratorium on governmental speeches concerning foreign
or military affairs and had General Marshall and me direct, on
presidential authority, that military commanders and diplomatic
representatives abroad must cease "direct communication on mili-

2. RAD JCS 97592, JCS to CINCFE, 29 Nov. 50; TEL CINCFE to JCS C50095,
30 Nov. 50; also RAD C50332 CINCUNC to DA for JCS, 3 Dec. 50, as seen in
Schnabel, *Policy and Direction*.
3. *Hearings on the Military Situation in the Far East*, p. 3492; for message to
Arthur Krock, see *ibid.*, p. 3496; for *U.S. News & World Report* interview, see
ibid., pp. 3532–33; for messages to United Press, see *ibid.*, pp. 3534–35.

tary or foreign policy with newspapers, magazines or other publicity media in the United States." [4] Aimed at MacArthur, this order was sent on December 6. "I should have relieved [him] then and there," the President wrote later.[5]

He himself had added to the confusion on November 30 by an unfortunate answer to a loaded press question about the use of atomic weapons in Korea, which brought Prime Minister Attlee scurrying across the ocean. We shall come to that visit shortly.

On December 1 a State-Defense meeting was again convened at the Pentagon. I pointed out that the contingency mentioned but not discussed at our last meeting—the failure of General Mac-Arthur's attack—was hard upon us. A state of panic seemed to exist at the United Nations; complaints were being made that U.S. leadership had failed; and disunity was observable in Asia and Europe. We must act to restore confidence and unity among our friends, which entailed coordinating military and political measures. There was no use in my going to the General Assembly until the United States had an agreed plan. The first questions were whether and where it was possible to hold a line, what political measures would help to stabilize the situation, and whether or not they should be started at this stage. If it was not possible to hold a line, a whole new set of questions arose that we should begin to examine, such as either extending the conflict or seeking for a way to end it. Here again, military and political measures must march together.

The upshot of a very full and frank discussion was that it was not possible to answer my questions yet. Indeed, so confused and confusing were the reports from headquarters that General Marshall asked General Collins to go at once himself and find out what was going on. Reinforcements were apparently coming to the Chinese from Manchuria; our troops were still too widely dispersed. We might have to fall much farther back and, unless the Eighth Army and X Corps could be united and regrouped, we might not be able to hold a line at all, but be forced into beachheads at Inchon, Wonsan, and Pusan. In such an eventuality, the possibility of holding the beachheads against possible Chinese and Russian bombing was doubtful. The use of nuclear weapons by us could lead to incalculable consequences. For the present, and unless the preservation of our troops required it, the balancing of the pros and cons of bombing Manchurian territory, including air and other bases, was against doing so. On this the Chiefs of Staff and civilian secretaries were unanimous.

4. *Hearings on the Military Situation in the Far East*, p. 3536.
5. Truman, *Years of Trial and Hope*, p. 384.

General MacArthur's other nostrums—blockading the China coast and using Nationalist troops from Formosa—were examined again and ruled out for both a tactical and strategic reason. At best they could be of only peripheral value. Furthermore, until we knew whether our forces would have to be evacuated from Korea or moved about by water, the Navy's fighting ships and transports should not be sent off on secondary missions. But even more basically the peripheral gain from these measures would put us on our own and lose us the great advantage of our UN position, leadership, and support.

Of the various political aids to battle—cease-fire, demilitarized zones, and so on—the only practicable and useful one seemed to be holding the United Nations to a condemnation of the Chinese, useful in itself and as a counteroffensive to Russian resolutions attacking our position regarding Formosa.

Washington Plans Next Moves

The next day, Saturday, was a busy one, working out among ourselves, then going over with General Marshall and together with the President, plans for our course at the United Nations. Ambassadors Warren Austin and Ernest Gross came down from New York to work with us. Suggestions of approaching the Chinese or the Russians with proposals for a cease-fire, either through Sir Benegal Rau or Sir Girja Bajpai of India or the Russians directly through our embassy, were vetoed. By the end of the afternoon the group had provided a memorandum for me to discuss with the President. I myself had to leave them to work on the forthcoming visit of Prime Minister Attlee.

Toward the end of the day, armed with satisfactory briefing notes and intelligence material on Chinese and Russian intentions, I set off for General Marshall's apartment to concert recommendations with him. Then with General Bradley we went to the President about eight o'clock, received his instructions, with which I returned to a group awaiting me in the Department. When the long day closed at ten o'clock, I went wearily home to a famished wife for sustenance, spiritous and solid.

The intelligence paper made these points: Chinese deployment and action in Manchuria and Korea were aimed to make the U.S.-UN position in Korea untenable. The attitude of the regime and the magnitude of military preparations in China itself indicated an appreciation of the risk of general war with the United States that this effort entailed. It was unlikely that the Chinese would have run this risk without some assurances of support from the Soviet Union. Support would probably include, in ascending order: continued provision of materiel, technicians, and perhaps, if necessary, "volunteers"; air units and anti-aircraft batteries for defense of targets in Manchuria should U.S.-UN air attack them; appropriate military support under the Sino-Soviet treaty in the event of U.S.-UN operations against other Chinese territory. Furthermore, the Soviet Union must have appreciated and decided to risk the increased danger of both general U.S.-Chinese war and global war, which Chinese intervention on the then existing scale might cause.

Finally, the Kremlin probably saw advantages to it in the U.S.-Chinese war flowing from the diversion, attrition, and containment of U.S. forces in an indecisive theater; the creation of conflict between the United States and her European allies and the obstruction of NATO plans; the disruption of UN unity against the original aggression in Korea, thus also aiding Communist objectives in Southeast Asia. If, however, the United States should decline the gamble of war with China and withdraw from Korea, the USSR might be counting on collecting the stakes in Korea and Indochina. In any event, the United States Government should expect aggressive Soviet pursuit of its attack on the world position of the United States. Other aggressions in Asia and Europe were not to be counted out.

Doubtless present-day "revisionist" writers would conclude that this paper and the agreement of the three of us with its conclusions as a guide to action represented "overreaction" to Communist action. Even with such help as hindsight gives—which I do not regard as much—I do not agree and am glad that we did not consider the conclusions overdrawn.

After discussing our recommendations for UN action in response to Chinese intervention, the President accepted some and rejected others. We were directed to put immediately on the agenda of the General Assembly an item with an accompanying memorandum raising the Chinese Communist intervention in Korea. It should leave open the action that we would urge after consultation with Attlee, who was arriving in thirty-six hours. We should, however, propose to him to renew in the General Assembly under the "Uniting for Peace" doctrine the resolution that the Soviet Union had vetoed in the Security Council and which combined assurance to China concerning its "legitimate interests" with an urgent appeal to desist from interference in Korea. Its provisions were not wholly appropriate to the changed fortunes of war, but it had the advantage of keeping our own position steady and calm and holding our UN allies together for a while, at least. The President wished us to

meet with the Chiefs of Staff first thing the next morning to consider latest developments and report to him again immediately
afterward. When all this was reported to my waiting colleagues,
I designated Jessup, Rusk, Matthews, and Nitze to go with me
and had a message sent to Harriman requesting his attendance.

Reports the next morning depicted MacArthur in a blue funk,
sorry for himself, complaining of the restrictions against expanding
the war, and sending to press and Pentagon what Lovett called
"posterity papers." He cabled the Pentagon on December 3 that
"this small command" was now facing an entire Chinese nation in
battle and called for reinforcements. Three days later he spelled
out his predicament statistically: "It is estimated that the Chinese
Communist forces [opposed to us in North Korea] now total
268,000. . . . In their rear, stretching back to and across the Yalu
River is . . . a minimum of 550,000 men. . . . The remainder
of Communist China constitutes another . . . reserve . . . about
4 million men under arms." [6] The Chiefs of Staff at once replied:
"We consider that the preservation of your forces is now the primary
consideration. Consolidation of forces into beachheads is concurred in."

The meetings of December 3 at the Pentagon and reported
at the White House took place amid deepening gloom. The generals told us that in two to three days the situation would reach
its crisis and, perhaps, a crash state. X Corps could and should be
evacuated, perhaps with heavy losses unless a cease-fire could be
arranged. It would rejoin the Eighth Army unless that, too, had to
be withdrawn. I opposed efforts to obtain a cease-fire until Mr.
Attlee had arrived and been consulted, and until the need for it
had become unmistakably clear. The Communist price for a cease-
fire could be very high indeed—perhaps too high for any *quid pro
quo* other than that of saving our forces. The least they would ask
would be withdrawal to the 38th parallel, but more probably from
all Korea, to which they might add abandonment of Formosa, and
a demand that the Conference of Foreign Ministers, with Communist China added, take over negotiation of a Japanese peace
treaty to diminish our influence in Japan.

General Marshall had raised the night before the dilemma

6. On November 17 Ambassador Muccio reported General MacArthur's view of
his operations in November. Not more than twenty-five thousand to thirty thousand
Chinese could get across the river without detection, if they continued the secrecy of
movement they were obviously practicing. The General would blow up the Korean
end of the Yalu bridges, leaving the surrounding area a desert. North Korea would
be cleared of hostile forces within ten days. He would then release all North Korean
prisoners and take all Chinese prisoners to the border, sending them back to Manchuria. The Eighth Army would return to Japan, leaving the X Corps, other national
contingents, and the South Korean forces to stabilize the situation.

that evacuation of Korea would pose between saving our troops and our national honor. We all agreed again that we could not in good conscience abandon the South Koreans to their Chinese-North Korean enemies. This made evacuation a last-ditch resort. Even a Dunkirk type of operation, General Marshall observed, would be hard if Sino-Soviet air entered the battle. I urged that the bombing of Manchurian airfields and territory also be considered as a last-ditch operation to be undertaken only if necessary to save our forces, and that the decision should not be left to General MacArthur but retained by the President and General Marshall with General Collins remaining at the front to report the facts. I had lost all faith in MacArthur's judgment.

At our meeting in the Pentagon General Ridgway, after pointing out on the map the course of the battle and listening to the usual discussion of the propriety of interference by Washington with the theater, asked to be allowed to state his own opinion. As he has written in his book, "I blurted out . . . that I felt we had already spent too damn much time on debate and that immediate action was needed. We owed it, I insisted, to the men in the field and to the God to whom we must answer for those men's lives to stop talking and to act." [7] This was the first time that someone had expressed what everyone thought—that the Emperor had no clothes on.

Finally turning to the domestic situation, I urged the President to declare the existence of a national emergency. Only in this way could the public be made aware of the seriousness of the situation and that the Government was fully alive to it. Furthermore, the President might soon need the powers the proclamation would bring him to control prices and wages and to establish far-reaching production controls. He indicated agreement.

Steady As You Go

Early the next morning I met Mr. Attlee's plane on the President's behalf, returning immediately to a small senior-staff meeting at the Department. There I found a short note from George Kennan, so wise and inspiring that I must quote it in full:

Dear Mr. Secretary:

There is one thing I would like to say in continuation of our discussion of yesterday evening. In international, as in private, life what counts most is not really what happens to someone but how he bears what hap-

7. Matthew B. Ridgway, *The Korean War* (New York: Doubleday & Company, 1967), p. 62.

pens to him. For this reason almost everything depends from here on
out on the manner in which we Americans bear what is unquestionably
a major failure and disaster to our national fortunes. If we accept it with
candor, with dignity, with a resolve to absorb its lessons and to make it
good by redoubled and determined effort—starting all over again, if necessary, along the pattern of Pearl Harbor—we need lose neither our self
confidence nor our allies nor our power for bargaining, eventually, with
the Russians. But if we try to conceal from our own people or from our
allies the full measure of our misfortune, or permit ourselves to seek relief
in any reactions of bluster or petulance or hysteria, we can easily find
this crisis resolving itself into an irreparable deterioration of our world
position—and of our confidence in ourselves.

George Kennan

I agreed enthusiastically and read it to the group, which included George himself. We were being infected, I said, by a spirit
of defeatism emanating from headquarters in Tokyo. How should
we begin to inspire a spirit of candor and redoubled and determined
effort? They all had good suggestions. Rusk said that the military
men were too dejected. They needed some of the do-or-die spirit
that had led the British in two world wars to hang on against overwhelming odds and with no visible hope of success. We had the
men, putting the divided forces together again, to take a terrible
toll from the Chinese, which was the best way to save both our
forces (by stopping the enemy or forcing a tolerable cease-fire)
and our position in Asia and Europe. He ended with a radical suggestion, the first foreshadowing of the future. Perhaps the President,
he threw out, would wish to think of placing General Collins in
supreme command in Korea and letting General MacArthur con-
centrate on his duties in Japan, including the peace treaty.

Kennan added that the worst possible time to negotiate with
the Communists was from a position of defeat. They would correctly interpret it as weakness; threats would only make them refuse
altogether to negotiate. Under Secretary Webb contributed that
the best way to start on a campaign to revive spirit in the Pentagon
was for me to talk with General Marshall.

I called him at once to ask him to discuss with Rusk and
Kennan an idea we had been talking over. The Korean campaign
had been cursed, I said, by violent swings between exuberant optimism and the deepest depression and despair. Both seemed to me
unwarranted. We had had enough logic and analysis; what we
needed was dogged determination to find a place to hold and fight
the Chinese to a standstill. This was a far better stance for the
United States than to talk about withdrawing from Korea or going

off on a policy of our own of bombing and blockading China. The General replied that he agreed, with two provisos: first, he must see with what success MacArthur got X Corps out of the east coast; second, we must not dig ourselves into a hole without an exit. I accepted the amendments and sent Rusk and Kennan to see him.

General Marshall repeated to them the conditions to making a stand he had stated to me, but Kennan pushed him. The State Department was not, he said, trying to determine military policy. If it was really true that an attempt to hold a beachhead would mean the loss of our entire forces or any other exorbitant consequence, that was that, and we had to accept it. But we must point out the political implications of this decision and make sure that they were borne in mind in whatever decision might be taken by the military authorities. Lovett, on joining the group, said that he had just come from Capitol Hill, where he and Admiral Forrest Sherman had been briefing the House Armed Services Committee. The prevailing feeling there seemed to him to have been that our entire entry into Korea had been a mistake and that we ought to pull out as rapidly as possible. General Marshall was not impressed. This sort of fluctuation in congressional opinion was not new to him. The present mood might not last for long.

Morale in the Pentagon was not improved by General Collins' first report from Tokyo of MacArthur's view that without either a cease-fire or a new policy of air attacks against and blockade of China, reinforcements from the United States and Formosa, and the possibility of using atomic weapons in North Korea, he would have to evacuate his forces.

My own plea to the country for steadiness in adversity had been made in a broadcast on the evening of November 29.[8] In it I described the full violence of the blows we were receiving in the field, as heavy as in the worst days of the desperate, last-ditch struggle about Pusan. No one could guarantee that a wider war would not come. The crisis was extremely serious. Whether reason would prevail was only partly for us to decide. We should hope and strive for the best while we prepared for the worst. The responsibility for doing this, for showing ourselves as a nation possessed of steadiness, moderation, restraint, constancy of purpose, and inflexibility in action, rested not only on members of the Government and the Congress but on every single American citizen. The nation was merely the sum total of these. It would show itself to the world bearing its ill fortunes and bettering them as its citizens showed themselves. Every individual must understand the forces

8. *Department of State Bulletin,* Vol. XXIII, December 18, 1950, pp. 962–67.

we were dealing with and the role required of us. No one could dodge that responsibility.

The moment I finished speaking the President was on the telephone to cheer and thank me.

The Attlee Visit

December opened by bringing us a Job's comforter in Clement Attlee, the British Labour Prime Minister. He was a far abler man than Winston Churchill's description of him as "a sheep in sheep's clothing" would imply, but persistently depressing. He spoke, as John Jay Chapman said of President Charles W. Eliot of Harvard, with "all the passion of a woodchuck chewing a carrot." His thought impressed me as a long withdrawing, melancholy sigh. The fright created in London when the British press misconstrued and exaggerated the unfortunate answers President Truman gave to questions at his press conference on November 30, 1950, propelled him across the ocean. This episode followed two earlier ones. In August Secretary of the Navy Francis P. Matthews in a speech in Boston called for preventive war. He was made Ambassador to Ireland. Then General Orville Anderson, Commandant of the Air War College, announced that the Air Force, equipped and ready, only awaited orders to drop its bombs on Moscow. He was retired.

In the course of the press conference mentioned above, the President had stated that "the forces of the United Nations have no intention of abandoning their mission in Korea." Then the questions began, illustrating vividly the dangers that lurk in the American press conference, with its stress on candid answers to questions that seem to be without guile. To one such the President answered that we would "take whatever steps are necessary to meet the military situation, just as we always have." Did that "include the atomic bomb?" It included "every weapon that we have." Had there been "active consideration of [its] use?" "There has always been active consideration of its use." Other questions, unconnected with the bomb, led to obviously correct answers that the application of appropriate weapons to appropriate targets lay within the province of the theater commander.[9] In London the House of Commons, engaged in a two-day foreign policy debate, received an erroneous report that General MacArthur might be given discretion to use the atomic weapons. Cries of alarm came from every quarter of the House, coupled with demands that before the die was cast the British must participate in deciding their fate. At the end of

9. *Public Papers of the Presidents, 1950*, pp. 724–28.

the debate the Prime Minister announced to cheers that he had cabled to the President his desire to fly to Washington for "a wide survey of the problems which face us today."

Meanwhile a damage-control party had gathered at the White House to prepare a "clarifying statement," issued within the hour:

The President wants to make it certain that there is no misinterpretation of his answers to questions at his press conference today about the use of the atom bomb. Naturally, there has been consideration of this subject since the outbreak of the hostilities in Korea, just as there is consideration of the use of all military weapons whenever our forces are in combat. Consideration of the use of any weapon is always implicit in the very possession of that weapon.

However, it should be emphasized, that, by law, only the President can authorize the use of the atom bomb, and no such authorization has been given. If and when such authorization should be given, the military commander in the field would have charge of the tactical delivery of the weapon.

In brief, the replies to the questions at today's press conference do not represent any change in this situation.[10]

Before the morning was much older, Sir Oliver Franks, the British Ambassador, received reassuring words and returned at the end of the afternoon with a telegram from Attlee. The Prime Minister wanted as soon as convenient to discuss with the President three items: the possible extension of the war in the Far East; raw-material supplies and their effect upon our joint ability to play our respective parts; and Western European defense. Asked whether the Prime Minister was seeking greater understanding of the situation and of our intentions or some form of agreements, which would need much more careful staff work here, Sir Oliver replied that the principal pressure was from the British domestic political situation and increasing public anxiety over present developments. He promised a clearer answer to my question and some suggested dates.

By coming to America the Prime Minister had not done with alarums and excursions. On the third morning of his visit, December 6, soon after my arrival at the Department, Deputy Secretary of Defense Lovett telephoned a report and an instruction from the President. Our early-warning radar system in Canada had picked up formations of unidentified objects, presumably aircraft, headed southeast on a course that could bring them over Washington in two or three hours. All interception and defense forces were alerted. I was to inform but not advise the Prime Minister. The Pentagon telephones would be closed for all but emergency defense purposes and he could not talk again. Before he hung up, I asked whether he believed that the objects picked up were Russian bombers. He said that he did not.

Getting Oliver Franks on the telephone, I repeated the message. He asked whether the President had canceled the eleven-thirty meeting with Attlee, and was told that he had not. We agreed to meet there. Before ending the talk, he wondered about the purpose of my message. I suggested fair warning and the opportunity for prayer. As we finished, one of our senior officials burst into the room. How he had picked up the rumor I do not know, perhaps from the Pentagon. He wanted to telephone his wife to get out of town, and to have important files moved to the basement. I refused to permit him to do either and gave him the choice of a word-of-honor commitment not to mention the matter to anyone or being put under security detention. He wisely cooled off and chose the former. When we reached the White House, Lovett told us that the unidentified objects had disappeared. His guess was that they had been geese.

In the State Department one never lacks helpful suggestions. Two days before Prime Minister Attlee arrived, one of these came from Bernard M. Baruch via Mr. Lovett as agent for his apparently reluctant chief, General Marshall. In Mr. Baruch's view the American people increasingly favored use of atomic weapons in Korea, though he and they were imprecise about where and against whom. In Mr. Baruch's opinion the President should convey the fact of this popular attitude to Mr. Attlee, regretfully, but not minimizing its strength. The stated purpose of doing so was to lead an alarmed Prime Minister to return to Europe to work out and insist upon some workable plan of appeasement in Korea, thus relieving the President, General Marshall, and me of the burden of doing so. Mr. Lovett declared that his only responsibility for this message was to deliver it; I wished him to note that my only response or responsibility was to listen to him do so.

Our five days of talks are not worth a day-by-day, play-by-play account. The chief impression they left with me was a deep dislike and distrust of the "summit conference" as a diplomatic instrument. Contrary to popular belief, Sir Winston Churchill and President Roosevelt did not invent it and, with perhaps two notable exceptions—the meetings of Münster and Osnabrück, which produced the Peace of Westphalia after the Thirty Years War (1648) and the Congress of Vienna (1814), and possibly the Congress of Berlin in 1878—it has not been successful. Although the summit may be high and therefore glamorous, some of its participants have often been ill prepared and others unreliable—or both, as in the case of the meeting of Francis I and Henry VIII at the Field of Cloth of Gold in 1520. The result has all too often been a gamble, the experience nerve-racking, and the results unsatisfactory. Philippe de Comines, a competent diplomatist, expressed the views of many of his latter-day colleagues that "two great Princes who wish to establish good personal relations should never meet each other face-to-face, but ought to communicate through good and wise ambassadors." [11] Frank I. Cobb counseled Colonel House in a memorandum of November 4, 1918, that "the moment President Wilson sits at the council table with these Prime Ministers and Foreign Secretaries he has lost all the power that comes from distance and detachment. . . . He becomes merely a negotiator dealing with other negotiators." [12]

When a chief of state or head of government makes a fumble, the goal line is open behind him. This I was to learn in my first experience with this dangerous diplomatic method, which has such attraction for American presidents.

The first purpose of the British group was to find out what was going on and why in North Korea. The explanation was entrusted to General Bradley, cross-examined by Field Marshal Sir William Slim, and took up most of our first day. The truth was hard to state and harder to believe. But Omar Bradley's patent integrity was equal to the first task, which he did not attempt to gloss. Before the meetings ended, General Collins had returned from the front and reported to the joint group. The long retreat had almost reached the 38th parallel. The prospect of extracting X Corps from the east coast appeared good. Generals Walker, MacArthur, and Collins all believed that a line south of Seoul could be held. The hysteria about evacuation had, temporarily at least, subsided.

As the Prime Minister became reassured that alarm over the safety of our troops would not drive us to some ill-considered use of atomic weapons, his purposes in coming emerged more clearly. He wished us to end our conflict with the Chinese in order to resume active participation in security for Europe; to resume also, as in the Second World War, a joint control with Britain of the allocation and pricing of raw materials, since the inevitable growth of rearmament would make them scarce and dear; and, finally, he

11. Quoted in Harold Nicolson, *The Evolution of Diplomatic Method* (London: Constable & Company, 1953), p. 43.
12. Herbert Hoover, *The Ordeal of Woodrow Wilson* (New York: McGraw-Hill, 1958), p. 62.

wished Britain to be admitted to some participation with us in any
future decision to use nuclear weapons. The Congress was not far
behind us in sensing that Mr. Attlee had not come here for a
lecture on current events. Indeed, while the conference was going
on, twenty-four Republican senators introduced and debated vigorously, but failed to pass, a resolution requiring ratification by the
Senate, as of a treaty, of any agreement made by the President and
Prime Minister. At the same time in New York and through the
American press our public was regaled by attacks upon the United
States from Soviet Ambassador Malik and special Chinese Communist envoy General Wu Hsiu-chuan. The General's presence
resulted from an invitation of the Security Council to discuss what
it politely termed the "new turn of events" in Korea. He chose
instead to join in support of Malik's resolutions condemning American "aggression" in Formosa and Korea. While our allies voted
these resolutions down, their high enthusiasm of the autumn had
evaporated, and none of them, including the British, would join
in a counteroffensive in the United Nations against Chinese intervention. The proceedings in both Washington and New York were
not helpful in rallying the country to meet major military reverses
and to bear the vagaries of a recalcitrant general. I wished then,
as often before and since, that the headquarters of the United
Nations were anywhere except in our own country.

Mr. Attlee's method of discussion was that of the suave rather
than the bellicose cross-examiner. He early noticed a tendency of
the President to show concurrence or the reverse in each statement
of his interlocutor as he went along. Framing his statements to
draw presidential agreement with his exposition, he soon led the
President well onto the flypaper. At the second meeting, as the
procedure started again, I stepped on the President's foot and suggested that it might be helpful to the Prime Minister to let him
complete his whole statement without interruption. It was far from
helpful to the Prime Minister, as his glance at me indicated, but
we fared better.

The line of Mr. Attlee's argument was that the position of
our forces in Korea was so weak and precarious that we must pay
for a cease-fire to extricate them. He believed that withdrawal from
Korea and Formosa and the Chinese seat in the United Nations
for the Communists would not be too high a price. There was
nothing, he warned us, more important than retaining the good
opinion of Asia. I remarked acidly that the security of the United
States was more important. President Truman and General Marshall
added that the preservation of our defenses in the western Pacific

and the belief of the Asian peoples in our fighting power were a path to securing their good opinion.

Intervening at the President's request, I gave the British comfort where they seemed entitled to it. The central opponent, I said, was not China but the Soviet Union. There had been foolish and irresponsible talk, repudiated by the Administration, for all-out war against China. Not many of the President's advisers would urge him to follow that course with the involvement it implied. On the other hand, the moment seemed to me the worst one for negotiation with the Russians since 1917. They saw themselves holding the cards and would concede nothing.

At the next meeting I suggested that Mr. Attlee would be making a serious mistake to believe that the American people would follow a leadership that proposed a vigorous policy of action against aggression on one ocean front while accepting defeat on the other. The public mind was not subtle enough to understand so ambivalent a policy, which was fortunate because it would be a wrong policy. Discussion of priorities was one thing; wholly different attitudes on the same issue on two sides of the world was another. We had with the almost unanimous approval of our allies gone after a small aggressor in Korea. Now a big one had come along and given us a licking. To cut, run, and abandon the whole enterprise was not acceptable conduct. The Chinese might be able to force it on us, but I doubted it. There was a great difference between being forced out and getting out. Upon this issue the President, General Marshall, and General Bradley moved up their big guns. After some exchanges on whether the Chinese were Soviet satellites or not and whether the Cairo declaration led logically to Formosa's going to the Chinese Communists, the engagement ended without any meeting of minds.

At the British Embassy after dinner on December 6, Field Marshal Slim and Marshal of the Air Force Lord Tedder said to me sorrowfully that their chief had muffed the ball I had passed to him during talks about European defense. They wished to have another try that evening and rounded up a group that included the President, the Prime Minister, Generals Marshall and Bradley, our host, and themselves. We talked from nine-thirty till after midnight.

Attlee, who apparently liked to operate behind a smoke screen, proceeded to get off the subject—US-UK policy toward European defense. He raised the "difficult and delicate question" of General MacArthur's conduct of the Korean war and absence of any allied say in what was done. Our two generals defended MacArthur and said that a war could not be run by a committee. The British had been consulted on matters tending to extend the war, such as the "hot pursuit" of enemy planes into Manchuria and the bombing of airfields there, and their views had been reflected in the action taken. The President added that since all involved had confided the unified command to the United States we would have to run it as long as that situation continued and we continued to supply so preponderantly the means and men to carry on the war. Supporting the President, I pleaded incompetence to discuss General MacArthur's military ability or judgment, but pointed out that so far as the strategic conduct of the war was concerned the Prime Minister and his advisers had been discussing that question for three days with our highest advisers, including the Commander in Chief himself. As I recalled, aside from the political purpose of ending the war as soon as possible, the Prime Minister had no criticism of the plan of campaign outlined to him. The President capped this rather bluntly by stating that we would stay in Korea and fight. If we had support from others, fine; if not, we would stay on anyway. On this note the Slim-Tedder second try sputtered out. However, they did noble work on the communiqué.

On the last day of the talks we had one of those close calls that lurk in summit meetings. General Collins had given his report from Korea. We were waiting in the Cabinet Room of the White House for a draft from the communiqué writers. The President had taken the Prime Minister to the privacy of his study. When secretaries distributed copies of the draft, our chiefs came back. They had, said the President cheerfully, been discussing the atomic weapon and agreed that neither of us would use these weapons without prior consultation with the other. No one spoke. The President asked the chief drafter to begin reading the communiqué for amendments. As he started, Lovett leaned over my shoulder to say that we were teetering on the edge of great trouble and that I must carry the ball. A whispered conversation with the President and a note passed across the table to Oliver Franks brought the three of us and the Prime Minister together in the President's office, while others continued revision of the draft.

I pointed out that over and over again the President had insisted that no commitment of any sort to anyone limited his duty and power under the law to authorize use of the atomic weapon if he believed it necessary in the defense of the country, and that he had gone far in declaring that he would not change that position. If he should attempt to change it, he would not be successful, since Congress would not permit it. The resolution of the twenty-four Republican senators gave fair warning of the temper of Congress. The suggestion he had made in the Cabinet Room would open a most vicious offensive against him and the British, whereas a program of keeping in close touch with the Prime Minister in all world situations that might threaten to move toward violence and hostilities of any kind would be widely approved.

All agreed with this, albeit Mr. Attlee a little sadly, and we began drafting a suitable paragraph, Oliver Franks acting as scribe. The President pulled out the slide at the left of his desk. Oliver left his chair and knelt between mine and Attlee's to write on it. "I think that this is the first time," said the President, "that a British Ambassador has knelt before an American President." Sir Oliver went right on drafting and produced a solution, which was inserted without comment in the communiqué when we returned to the Cabinet Room: "The President stated that it was his hope that world conditions would never call for the use of the atomic bomb. The President told the Prime Minister that it was also his desire to keep the Prime Minister at all times informed of developments which might bring about a change in the situation." [13]

The communiqué ended my first summit conference, accompanied by an ungranted prayer that I might be spared another, and by the grateful recognition of the gap between Mr. Attlee's brief and the consent decree—to use lawyers' terms—that he had signed.

Congressional and public response to the communiqué was, on the whole, good. In the Senate committee the two senior members, Connally and Wiley, stalwart soldiers and sensible men, carried the others along in a statement, after my meeting with them, that pretty well concluded the fuss. There was little to add, they said, to so complete a communiqué. One thing was clear to them —that the British and American positions were "substantially closer than would have appeared a week ago." If ever a true word was spoken this was it. Senator Knowland was, of course, "shocked"; he saw "the making of a Far Eastern Munich contained in its language." President Syngman Rhee strangely thought that "it would have been better if the United Nations had not helped us at all if we are to be abandoned now." However, the furor that the announcement of the Attlee visit had kicked up fizzled out and was soon forgotten.

13. *Department of State Bulletin*, Vol. XXIII, December 18, 1950, p. 961.

V

ATTEMPTS TO STABILIZE
THE WAR

To STABILIZE the Korean war involved nearly simultaneous efforts
on three separate fronts: the front in Korea, the front in the United
Nations, and the front in Tokyo. The most intractable was the last.

On the Korean Front

An event of incalculable importance occurred on December
23, 1950, though we in Washington—that is, we civilians—did
not recognize it as such. General Walton Walker, commanding the
Eighth Army, was killed when his jeep crashed on an icy Korean
road and Major General Matthew B. Ridgway was appointed to
succeed him. Two days later—measured by Korean time—General
Ridgway reported to General MacArthur and took over command
of the Eighth Army, soon to be joined by X Corps. General
MacArthur concluded their meeting, as General Ridgway has told
us, by saying, "The Eighth Army is yours, Matt. Do what you
think best."

He never uttered wiser words. Within a month the longest
retreat in American history ended and the Army, its fighting spirit
restored, "started rolling forward," to use its commander's words.[1]
Temporarily checked by a heavy Chinese counterattack in mid-
February, the advance continued with Operation Killer on March 7,
designed primarily—as its name indicates—to inflict heavy losses
on the Chinese, which it did. On March 15 Seoul was retaken,
not to be lost again, and by April 9 the Army was established on

1. Ridgway, *The Korean War*, pp. 83, 106.

the Kansas line north of the 38th parallel, where General Ridgway held it concentrated, coordinated, and urgently preparing to
meet another Chinese offensive that appeared to be in the making.
Both he and Washington were confident that the Army could
absorb all the Chinese could throw at us and were clear that there
was to be no more talk of withdrawal from Korea unless the Soviet
Union should intervene in strength, which we deemed unlikely.

On the United Nations Front

Our last glimpse of the scene in New York was one of some
confusion. Soviet Ambassador Jacob Malik and special Chinese
Communist envoy General Wu Hsiu-chuan were attacking the
United States for its stand on Korea and Formosa, we were trying
to rally our friends to vote a condemnation of Chinese aggression
in Korea, and the Indians and others were striving for a cease-fire
resolution. Since the United Nations was one of the belligerents,
a cease-fire resolution would be obviously an appeal by the weaker
to the stronger side. For this reason the United States Government in the current military situation would neither participate
in the effort nor block it. The Chinese, however, did the latter.
General Wu declared illegal a resolution asking Nasrollah Entezam
of Iran, President of the Assembly, and two associates to determine
the basis on which a cease-fire could be arranged, and Chou En-lai
announced that as "the only acceptable basis for negotiation" of a
peaceful settlement in Korea all foreign troops must be withdrawn
and the domestic affairs of Korea left to Koreans; that American
forces must be "withdrawn" from Formosa; and that the Chinese
Communist Government must be seated in the United Nations.[2]
Mr. Entezam reported failure on January 2.

Not content with this rebuff, the British, Canadians, Indians,
and others produced another bid to the Chinese, a resolution pro-
posing five principles for peaceful settlement in Korea: (1) a cease-
fire; (2) a political meeting for restoring peace; (3) a withdrawal
by stages of all foreign forces; (4) arrangements for an immediate
administration of all Korea; (5) a conference, after a cease-fire,
of the United Kingdom, the United States, the Soviet Union, and
the Chinese Communists to discuss Far Eastern problems, including the future of Formosa and the representation of China in the
United Nations.

The choice whether to support or oppose this plan was a
murderous one, threatening, on one side, the loss of the Koreans

2. *The New York Times,* December 23, 1950.

and the fury of Congress and press and, on the other, the loss
of our majority and support in the United Nations. We chose,
after painful deliberation in the Department—and after I recommended to the President what may well have been, even without
hindsight, the wrong alternative—to support the resolution. We
did so in the fervent hope and belief that the Chinese would
reject it (as they did) and that our allies would then return (as
they did) to comparative sanity and follow us in censuring the
Chinese as aggressors. The President—bless him—supported me
in even this anguishing decision. At once the political roof fell
in, Senator Taft attacked us with great violence, and a new facet
was added to the great debate over our foreign-policy objectives in
which the Senate was already engaged. Fortunately the storm soon
blew itself out. The resolution proposed on January 11 and adopted
on the thirteenth was rejected four days later by the Chinese. Our
allies—rather grudgingly, as they believed that the United States
was getting the best of both worlds when the State Department
supported the five principles and the country rejected them—
joined us on February 1 in passing a condemnation of Chinese
aggression but dragged their feet until May in taking any action
to punish the aggressor.

Thus the United Nations front fell into restless stability, disturbed by echoes of the irrepressible conflict in progress between
Washington and Tokyo.

On the Tokyo Front

When the Chinese attacks exploded all around his forces in
North Korea late in November, General MacArthur cabled to the
Chiefs of Staff that all hope of localizing the Korean conflict had
gone. The Chinese wanted, he said, the complete destruction of
his forces; they could be saved only by carrying the war to China.
To General Collins in Tokyo he characterized as essentially a policy
of surrender a refusal to authorize air attacks on China, a naval
blockade of the China coast, reinforcements from Formosa, or a
consideration of atomic bombing in North Korea. At the same time,
as already noted, he complained to the press of "an enormous
handicap without precedent in military history," in which he included the ban on "hot pursuit" of enemy aircraft into Manchuria
and the "privileged sanctuary" provided the Chinese by refusal
to permit bombing of Manchurian airfields and military targets.
He did not, however, note our own counterbalancing sanctuaries
in South Korea.

On the day after Christmas the President summoned Secretary of the Treasury Snyder, Generals Marshall and Bradley, and myself to a strategy meeting at Blair House. It was a long one. I proposed a rewriting and clarification of General MacArthur's directives. The stakes in Korea were so high that the United Nations should not withdraw until we had tested Chinese strength fully and found that dire military necessity required it. General MacArthur should not be required to defend any particular line but to inflict the maximum losses on the enemy by the use of air, sea, and land power, including Korean forces (the strategy later adopted by General Ridgway). He should not risk the destruction of his troops, since on them lay the ultimate responsibility for the defense of Japan. The generals saw an increased threat of general war and were clear that it should not be fought in Korea. They agreed to the rewriting of the directive, and the President authorized it.

The next day a draft was discussed by the Generals with the President and me and sent off on December 29. It stated: [3]

Chinese Communists now appear, from estimates available, capable of forcing evacuation by forces of UN. By committing substantial United States forces which would place other commitments, including safety of Japan, in serious jeopardy, or by inflicting serious losses on him, enemy might be forced to abandon exercise of his capability. If with present UN strength successful resistance at some position in Korea without our incurring serious losses could be accomplished and apparent military and political prestige of Chinese Communists could be deflated, it would be of great importance to our national interests. In the face of increased threat of general war JCS believe commitment of additional United States ground forces in Korea should not be made, since our view is that major war should not be fought in Korea.

Not considered practicable to obtain at this time significant additional forces from other United Nations. Therefore in light of present situation your basic directive, of furnish to ROK assistance as necessary to repel armed attack and restore to the area security and peace, is modified. Your directive now is to defend in successive positions, subject to safety of your troops as your primary consideration, inflicting as much damage to hostile forces in Korea as is possible.

In view of continued threat to safety of Japan and possibility of forced withdrawal from Korea it is important to make advance determination of last reasonable opportunity for orderly evacuation. It appears here that if Chinese Communists retain force capability of forcing evacuation after having driven UN forces to rear it would be necessary to direct commencement of your withdrawal. Request your views on these conditions which

3. Paraphrase of the summary of the message sent by the Joint Chiefs of Staff to General Douglas MacArthur on December 29, 1950. *Hearings on the Military Situation in the Far East*, pp. 2179–80.

should determine evacuation. You should consider your mission of defending Japan and limitation on troops available to you. Definite directive on
conditions for initiation of evacuation will be provided when your views
are received.

For the present—this message which has been handled with ultimate
security should be known only to your chief of staff and to Ridgway and
his chief of staff.

General MacArthur's views were requested on the conditions which
should determine evacuation.[4]

General MacArthur has recorded his views on receiving this
message: it seemed to him "to indicate a loss of 'will to win' in
Korea"; it was "unrealistic" because it offered no reinforcements,
and it was "especially fantastic" in expecting the Eighth Army
to be responsible for the defense of Japan.[5] On the same day
(December 30) he put forward four recommendations: to blockade
the coast of China; to destroy China's industrial capacity by bombing; to use Nationalist Chinese troops in Korea; to encourage action
by Formosa against the Chinese mainland. Barring these actions
and without reinforcement, withdrawal to Pusan was the only way
evacuation of Korea could be effected—a course that he attributed
to the Chiefs of Staff.[6] On January 9, 1951, the Chiefs repeated
their order to defend in successive positions, inflicting maximum
losses on the enemy, and that MacArthur's primary consideration
should be the safety of his troops and the defense of Japan.[7] In
case of necessity to achieve either of these, he was authorized to
withdraw to Japan. His suggestions, they said, were under consideration but they pointed out the major objections to adopting
them. This portion of the reply was to be used later by General
MacArthur and his apologists as evidence that the Chiefs agreed
with the recommendations (which they did not), but that I and
others torpedoed them.

At this point MacArthur attempted to put a squeeze on the
Chiefs. He "shot a query right back"—in his own phrase.[8] It was
self-evident, he cabled, that his command was incapable of holding
a position in Korea and at the same time protecting Japan against
external attack. He referred to the bad morale of his troops. (When
General Marshall read this, he remarked to Dean Rusk that when

---

4. RAD JCS 99935 JCS Personal to MacArthur, 30 Dec. 50, seen in Schnabel,
Policy and Direction.
5. MacArthur, *Reminiscences,* p. 378.
6. *Hearings on the Military Situation in the Far East,* pp. 2180–81; also, Mac-
Arthur, *Reminiscences,* pp. 378–80.
7. Truman, *Years of Trial and Hope,* pp. 433–34, and JCS 80680 JCS Personal
to MacArthur, 9 Jan. 51, as seen in Schnabel, *Policy and Direction.*
8. MacArthur, *Reminiscences,* p. 380.

a general complains of the morale of his troops, the time has come to look into his own.) The Government must decide on grounds of high policy which it was to do. "Under the extraordinary limitations and conditions imposed upon the command in Korea, as I have pointed out, its military position is untenable, but it can hold, if overriding political considerations so dictate, for any length of time up to its complete destruction. Your clarification requested." [9]

Here was a posterity paper if there ever was one, with the purpose not only of clearing MacArthur of blame if things went wrong but also of putting the maximum pressure on Washington to reverse itself and adopt his proposals for widening the war against China. Nothing further was needed to convince me that the General was incurably recalcitrant and basically disloyal to the purposes of his Commander in Chief. Deeply disturbed, I was not then aware that General Ridgway was to save the situation from disaster. After a hasty series of meetings, including one of the National Security Council, the President with infinite patience decided on another attempt by three messages to get through to the Supreme Commander the purposes and problems of the United States Government. He also dispatched Generals J. Lawton Collins and Hoyt S. Vandenberg to Korea to report back on what the actual situation was, stripped of MacArthur's colorful rhetoric. For purposes of clarity each of the messages dealt with a separate facet of the Korean problem in the hope that MacArthur, too, would keep them separate—a vain hope.

In the first of the messages, the Chiefs repeated their current operating directive (for the third time).[10] "Based upon all the factors known to us, including particularly those presented by you in your present message," it appeared to the Chiefs "infeasible under existing conditions" to hold the position in Korea for a protracted period. However, it would be to the interest of the United States and the United Nations to gain some further time for military and diplomatic consultation before beginning evacuation. Therefore, the Chiefs stressed the importance of inflicting "maximum practicable punishment" on the enemy and of not evacuating Korea "unless actually forced by military considerations."

In their second message, of January 12, 1951, delivered personally by General Collins (and read by him to General MacArthur to insure his getting it direct and not through some staff interpretation), the Chiefs discussed what might be done should the situation worsen *and the UN Command be forced to evacuate*

Korea.[11] Sixteen possible actions, including General MacArthur's four, all or some of which might be taken after evacuation, were put forward for study in preparation for military and diplomatic consultations. The Chiefs had "tentatively" approved them for this purpose. General Marshall had not; neither had I. We were to discuss them in the National Security Council with the President on January 17. By that date, however, Generals Vandenberg and Collins had returned from Korea and reported a wholly changed situation. The morale of the Army was good, and Ridgway was preparing to take the initiative. He did not feel hampered by the restrictions against operations outside of Korea. It was his and their opinion, in which—*mirabile dictu!*—MacArthur now concurred ("No one is going to drive us into the sea," he announced [12]), that short of active Soviet intervention the Army could continue operations in Korea without endangering its security as long as the national interest required. The Chinese were now having their own difficulties.

The sixteen possible actions for study never went farther. Nevertheless, General MacArthur was "gratified," his Chief of Staff has reported, "to learn that . . . the Joint Chiefs of Staff had finally overcome their illusions that fighting back against China would bring on global war" and had advised the carrying out of his recommendations.[13]

Generals Marshall and Bradley joined me in urging the President that he, rather than Chiefs of Staff—with whom General MacArthur would argue—should send him a third message setting out authoritatively "our basic national and international purposes" in Korea. It was an imaginatively kind and thoughtful letter for the Chief of State to write his theater commander, admitting him to his private mind.[14] The President worked hard and long over a rough draft we had prepared for him. He began by assuring the General that the situation in Korea was receiving his "utmost attention," and then listed ten specific purposes to which continued resistance to aggression would contribute; stressed the necessity of consolidating and holding our support in the United Nations as a strong deterrent to Soviet intervention and, for the same reason, of avoiding widening the war; referred to the adverse possibilities against which he was urgently increasing our military strength; and ended with generous praise of General MacArthur's "splendid lead-

11. For text with deletions, see *ibid.*, pp. 333–34.
12. *Washington Post,* January 21, 1951.
13. *Hearings on the Military Situation in the Far East,* p. 13; Whitney, *MacArthur: His Rendezvous with History,* p. 462.
14. Truman, *Years of Trial and Hope,* pp. 435–36.

ership" and the "superb performance" of his forces. If ever a message should have stirred the loyalty of a commander, this one should have done so.

Within a month, however, exculpations and complaints began again. The future in Korea, the General complained on February 13, depended on "international considerations and decisions not yet known here." His own field strategy upon Chinese intervention, consisting of a rapid withdrawal, lengthening the enemy's supply lines, and "pyramiding of his logistical difficulties" by "an almost astronomical increase" of air bombardment, had worked well. But he still suffered from the enemy's "unprecedented military advantage of sanctuary protection for his military potential against our counterattack upon Chinese soil." [15] Generals Vandenberg and Collins had reported that this was not the case. Once again MacArthur was refused authority to attack Chinese territory.

The Parallel Once More

While General MacArthur was fighting the Pentagon, General Ridgway was fighting the enemy. The Eighth Army, joined by X Corps, its fighting spirit restored, its fire power concentrated and greatly increased, took the offensive. General Ridgway held it, to use a term of horsemanship, tightly collected. Its mission was not to recover territory but to destroy enemy forces. This it did with terrible efficiency, even falling back before enemy offensives to lead him into prepared fields of fire. Relentlessly the Army moved north and, once again, approach to the parallel brought new policy discussions between the Department and Ambassador Muccio and across the Potomac between State and Defense.

Two memoranda and meetings between high officers of both departments reveal a situation that was the exact reverse of criticisms made at the time and later by partisan political sources as well as by academicians. It has been charged both that the State Department dominated or tried to dominate the military conduct of the war and that the Chiefs of Staff did the same in the diplomatic and political field. In fact, both charges were wrong and the truth was quite the opposite. Memoranda from State, dated February 13 and 23, 1951, and meetings of the same dates make plain the position of each department that it could not make definitive recommendations in its own field without conclusions of the other. Indeed, so insistent was each upon having guidance from the other that it gave rise to some sharp expressions suggesting avoidance of

15. *Hearings on the Military Situation in the Far East,* p. 3539.

responsibilities. The later paper, a tentative approach of my own for General Marshall, was rather tartly described by the Chiefs as "an unsound approach," since State should first formulate the political objectives before the Chiefs could devise the military means to achieve them. This is worth noting in connection with a commonly held view that the two departments were in a constant struggle for domination. Conflict was not unknown, as these pages amply show; but when the going was tough each showed great deference to the other in the assumption of responsibility.

In the end we found ourselves agreed on some fairly simple and sensible conclusions. To begin with, and despite some illusions to the contrary, United Nations and United States war aims had not included the unification of Korea by armed force against all comers, and Chinese intervention had now removed this as a practical possibility. The aim was to repulse the aggression and to bring about such a condition of stability that the large UN army could be withdrawn by stages and a line held against the North Koreans by a rearmed and competent Korean Army. The ultimate political aim—a Korea united by peaceful means—though clearly remote, should be retained. The line to be sought and held should be north of the parallel and chosen for its tactical defensive possibilities and practicality of attainment. As April opened, General Ridgway entered the area over which he was to fight for two years, continually weakening and bleeding the enemy without risking his Army, a mission regarding which he and his Government were in complete accord. In this area he found and held the line which became that of the ultimate cease-fire.

The Final Showdown

"Whom the gods destroy they first make mad," wrote Euripides.

Early in March 1951 General MacArthur's communications revealed surprise and pique over General Ridgway's success in executing the Government's purposes and strategy with the forces available to him. This MacArthur contemptuously called an "accordion" war. Chinese aggression, he believed, according to his Chief of Staff, "could not be stopped by killing Chinese" [16]—although in fact it was. Unless the enemy's war potential was opened to counterattack, he stated publicly on March 7, 1951, the battle lines would in time "reach a point of theoretical military

16. Whitney, *MacArthur: His Rendezvous with History*, p. 462.

stalemate." [17] He seemed both unable and unwilling to understand that General Ridgway was seeking to establish such a battle line at an advantageous and defensible point as the first step in ending the aggression and the war. He called for decision at the "highest international levels" to provide "an answer to the obscurities which now becloud the unsolved problems raised by Red China's undeclared war in Korea."

On March 15 the General took a step beyond private harassment of the Government. Openly defying the President's order of December 6 to military commanders forbidding unauthorized statements to the press, he gave one to Hugh Baillie, President of the United Press.[18] It criticized stopping the Eighth Army's advance at the 38th parallel or short of "accomplishment of our mission in the unification of Korea." He had been told over and over again that this was not his mission.

Nine days later he perpetrated a major act of sabotage of a Government operation. For some time we had been discussing within the Government and with our allies an idea strongly held in the General Assembly that further diplomatic efforts toward settlement should be made before major forces moved north of the parallel. The idea crystallized in favor of a statement to be made by the President on behalf of the unified command stating that there was a basis for peace in Korea and that the UN Command was prepared to enter into arrangement for a cease-fire to open the way for a broader settlement. On March 21 a draft approved by the President was submitted to the governments participating with troops in Korea. Their responses were favorable. On March 20 the Chiefs of Staff informed General MacArthur of what was in the wind and asked whether he had "sufficient freedom of action for next few weeks" to provide for the security of his forces and keeping contact with the enemy.[19] He replied that he had.

At eleven o'clock on the evening of March 23, Deputy Secretary of Defense Robert Lovett, with Alexis Johnson, Dean Rusk, and Lucius Battle of the State Department, came to me with a pronunciamento that General MacArthur had issued that morning (March 24 in Tokyo). Bob, usually imperturbable and given to ironic humor under pressure, was angrier than I had ever seen him. The General, he said, must be removed and removed at once. After reading the statement I shared his sense of outrage. It can be de-

17. *Hearings on the Military Situation in the Far East*, pp. 3540–41.
18. *New York Herald Tribune*, March 16, 1951.
19. *Hearings on the Military Situation in the Far East*, p. 411.

scribed only as defiance of the Chiefs of Staff, sabotage of an operation of which he had been informed, and insubordination of the
grossest sort to his Commander in Chief. We discussed it and its
consequences until one o'clock.

MacArthur's statement [20] began with a paragraph of bombastic
self-praise of his brilliance in defeat, followed by one of denigration
of the enemy. China's "exaggerated and vaunted military power"
lacked the necessary industrial base for modern war. Its military
weakness had been revealed even against a force under the inhibitions from which he suffered. The Chinese would never conquer
Korea, he wrote, and if his inhibitions were lifted and their coastal
areas and interior bases struck, they would be doomed to military
collapse. Once these basic facts were recognized, the Korean problem no longer "burdened by extraneous matters . . . such as
Formosa and China's seat in the United Nations" would not be
difficult to solve. MacArthur, as the UN commander, would be
willing to confer in the field with the enemy commander to find
military means whereby the political objectives of the United Nations could be realized.

When, the next morning, the President called Lovett, Rusk,
and myself to the White House, Lovett had simmered down. The
President, although perfectly calm, appeared to be in a state of
mind that combined disbelief with controlled fury. Asking first
whether his order of December 6, 1950, was clear to us and being
assured that it was, he dictated a message to MacArthur which laid
so plainly the foundation for a court-marshal as to give pause even
to General MacArthur:

The President has directed that your attention be called to his order
as transmitted 6 December, 1950. In view of the information given you
20 March 1951 any further statements by you must be coordinated as
prescribed in the order of 6 December.

The President has also directed that in the event Communist military
leaders request an armistice in the field, you immediately report that fact
to the JCS for instructions.[21]

MacArthur's career as an independent spokesman to the public or the enemy was obviously coming to an end. In his memoirs
President Truman has written that this act of MacArthur's left him
no choice; that he could no longer tolerate his insubordination; and
that he had already made up his mind before the last straw was laid
on his patience.[22] I have no doubt of it, but can add that he said

20. *Hearings on the Military Situation in the Far East*, pp. 3541–42.
21. Truman, *Years of Trial and Hope*, p. 443.
22. *Ibid.*, pp. 441–45.

no word of his decision to me nor, so far as I know, to anyone else. When the next incident occurred on April 5, it took the form of the revelation of a statement made before the order of March 24 and falling outside flat disobedience of a direct order of a superior officer.

To Joseph W. Martin of Massachusetts, Minority Leader of the House of Representatives, General MacArthur had written on March 20 agreeing with Mr. Martin's view that, contrary to his superiors' decision, the UN Command should use Nationalist Chinese forces in the Korean war.[23]

The General then proceeded, addressing the leader of the opposition, to a direct attack on the President's policies as he had explained them in his personal message a week earlier: "It seems strangely difficult for some to realize that here in Asia is where the Communist conspirators have elected to make their play for global conquest, and that we have joined the issue thus raised on the battlefield; that here we fight Europe's war with arms, while the diplomats there still fight it with words; that if we lose this war to Communism in Asia the fall of Europe is inevitable; win it and Europe most probably would avoid war and yet preserve freedom. As you pointed out, we must win. There is no substitute for victory."

On April 5 Mr. Martin released this letter, an open declaration of war on the Administration's policy, and read it in the House. Also on April 5 the *London Daily Telegraph* published a dispatch from Hong Kong relating an interview allegedly given to its Military Correspondent, Lieutenant General H. G. Martin, by General MacArthur, who was quoted as saying that "United Nations forces were circumscribed by a web of artificial conditions. . . . He found himself in a war without a definite objective. . . . It was not the soldier who had encroached upon the realm of the politician [but the other way around]. . . . The true object of a commander in war was to destroy the forces opposed to him. But this was not the case in Korea. The situation would be ludicrous if men's lives were not involved."

Senator Homer Ferguson, Republican of Michigan, proposed that a congressional committee should go to Tokyo and ascertain directly from the General his views on how the war should be run. When a request came from the President to meet with him and General Marshall immediately after the Cabinet the next morning, April 6, I was in little doubt what the subject of our discussion would be.

23. *Hearings on the Military Situation in the Far East*, p. 3544.

VI

THE RELIEF OF
GENERAL MAC ARTHUR

The Days of Decision

After the Cabinet meeting on Friday morning, April 6, General Bradley and Averell Harriman joined General Marshall and me in the President's office. The President asked and we discussed for about an hour what should be done about General MacArthur's open defiance of him. From the moment of reading the telegram to Congressman Martin my mind was clear on the nature of the problem. It was not so much what should be done as how it should be done. The situation could be resolved only by relieving the General of all his commands and removing him from the Far East. Grave trouble would result, but it could be surmounted if the President acted upon the carefully considered advice and unshakable support of all his civilian and military advisers. If he should get ahead of them or appear to take them for granted or be impetuous, the harm could be incalculable.

As we talked the matter over, it became very clear to me that Generals Marshall and Bradley would need time for unhurried discussion with the Chiefs of Staff, free from any pressure from prior conclusions, even tentative ones, expressed by the Commander in Chief. The Chiefs were out of town and could not be reassembled for deliberation and recommendation until the weekend. My whole effort, therefore, was to keep discussion going and conclusions at bay until all views could be in and all persons committed. There was no doubt what General MacArthur deserved; the sole issue was the wisest way to administer it.

In the afternoon of the same day General Marshall, Averell Harriman, and General Bradley met in my office for further discussion. Either then or in the morning General Marshall asked our opinion on the merits of calling General MacArthur home for consultation and reaching final decision after that. We were all strongly opposed. To me this seemed a road to disaster. The effect of MacArthur's histrionic abilities on civilians and of his prestige upon the military had been often enough demonstrated. To get him back in Washington in the full panoply of his commands and with his future the issue of the day would not only gravely impair the President's freedom of decision but might well imperil his own future. General Marshall, who had not pressed the idea, was convinced.

We four met again briefly with the President on Saturday morning, when General Bradley reported that the Chiefs were returning to town and would be ready for continuous sessions over Sunday. We were dismissed to meet again on Monday morning, with our matured and final recommendation. However, I was summoned again, and this time alone, on Sunday morning. The President told me that he had drawn John Snyder, Secretary of the Treasury, into the circle of his advisers on this matter, but had expressed no conclusion. I urged him to continue his very wise course of not disclosing the trend of his thoughts until all recommendations were in and he was ready to decide and act. Whatever his action, all of us would be examined and questioned. On one matter we should all be clear and under no necessity to plead privilege: for the President should never intimate to any of us his opinion and intended action until, having heard the recommendations of all the responsible civilian and military officers, he should announce his decision.

To the group assembled once more in the President's study on Monday morning, April 9, General Marshall announced that the Chiefs of Staff, having met under the chairmanship of General Bradley, unanimously recommended that General MacArthur be relieved of all his commands and that both he and General Bradley concurred in the recommendation. Averell and I, asked for our views, concurred. The President said that he was of the same opinion and asked whether the generals had a recommendation for a successor to General MacArthur. They proposed and the President accepted Lieutenant General Matthew B. Ridgway, which delighted both Harriman and me. We were all asked to return the next day with the draft orders to put these decisions into effect.

The Communications Mix-up

The orders and other necessary papers were given to me by the President on Tuesday afternoon to be sent through our code to Ambassador Muccio in Pusan for delivery to Secretary of the Army Frank Pace, who was at the front. Pace was instructed to fly at once to Tokyo and present them to General MacArthur. We had discussed the method of delivery and concluded that the one just described would save the General the embarrassment of direction transmission through Army communications, with the inevitable leaks of such interesting news. Unfortunately something went wrong with the commercial cable line through which the Department had to transmit. By midnight, although the cable company insisted that delivery had been made in Pusan, we had heard nothing from Muccio, who had been instructed to reply in clear "cable received" upon receipt. Thereupon the President and General Bradley, having heard rumors of press inquiries, dispatched the orders direct through the Army's own system. In Tokyo this was believed, quite mistakenly, to have been an unnecessary affront to General MacArthur.

Meanwhile our message was received in Pusan, decoded, and telephoned to Pace, who was with Ridgway in his headquarters tent. Pace later told me that he received the message during a hailstorm, when the noise in the tent was like that inside a drum when vigorously beaten. He and Ridgway took the instrument outside to pick up enough of the amazing message to send them scurrying off to Pusan to get it straight and then on to Tokyo, from which the General returned immediately to await his relief, General James A. Van Fleet.

In Washington my day was not notably more relaxed. On Tuesday afternoon after the orders had been sent to the code room, I kept a strange appointment on Capitol Hill with Senators Pat McCarran of Nevada and Styles Bridges of New Hampshire. This was a product of quite a diplomatic negotiation. Our relations had been so strained that they were not sure that I would receive them if they asked for an appointment, so they asked Deputy Under Secretary Carlisle Humelsine to sound me out. To their surprise I said I would be delighted to call on them, which I did. After wholly insincere cordiality on both sides, they disclosed their purpose. The President, they feared, was headed for an ill-considered row with General MacArthur, which he was sure to lose. The General's view would have great support in Congress and the President's would not. They pressed me to get the President to reconsider his attitude and come to an accommodation with the General. I told them that the President would be deeply interested in the views of such distinguished and influential senators, which I would faithfully report —as I did. Of course, when the next day's news of the relief broke, they accused me of misleading them by silence—a charge not without some justification, though no other course was possible —and our relations deteriorated further.

With the change in the communications channels, a busy night opened before us. Shortly after midnight my two secretaries, Luke Battle and Barbara Evans, arrived at my house and telephoning began. I spoke to Senators Tom Connally of Texas and Robert Kerr of Oklahoma, who had great influence, and to Leslie Biffle, Secretary of the Senate, and Boyd Crawford, Clerk of the House Committee on Foreign Affairs, asking them to speak on my behalf to such members of the Senate and House, respectively, as they thought wise, leaving old Judge Kee, Chairman of the House committee, who had a bad heart, until morning. We then went through the ambassadors of states that had troops in Korea under MacArthur's command.

I also got Foster Dulles out of bed and over to see me. He was dismayed by the news and even more dismayed to learn that the President wanted him to go at once to Tokyo to reassure Prime Minister Shigeru Yoshida that no change in policy toward Japan or the treaty would result. He must have time, he said, to consult with Senator Taft and others. I told him to get on with it, to be ready to start within a day or so, and to go with me the next day to the White House, where the President would give him a message for Mr. Yoshida. (He was airborne in thirty-six hours.)

A day or two later at the next Cabinet meeting the President asked me to give my impression of the events of the last few days. It was summed up, I said, by the story of the family with the beautiful young daughter who lived on the edge of a large army camp. The wife worried continually, and harassed her husband, over the dangers to which this exposed their daughter. One afternoon the husband found his wife red-eyed and weeping on the doorstep. The worst had happened, she informed him; their daughter was pregnant! Wiping his brow, he said, "Thank God that's over!"

We settled down to endure the heavy shelling from press and Congress that the relief was bound to and did produce. The General returned to the United States and a hero's welcome, made a

General MacArthur had been relieved of his duties. He returned as though he were a conquering hero. He is shown here parading in New York City April 20, 1951. WIDE WORLD

General MacArthur before a joint session of Congress in a speech wherein he uttered his famous line, "Old soldiers never die. They just fade away." WARDER COLLECTION

demagogic speech to Congress and—via television—to the country, and appeared on May 3, 1951, before the Senate Committees on Armed Services and Foreign Relations as the first witness in their "Inquiry into the Military Situation in the Far East and the Facts Surrounding the Relief of General of the Army Douglas MacArthur from his Assignments in that Area." This inquiry, conducted with great skill for eight weeks by Senator Richard Russell of Georgia, Chairman, exhausted both committees, bored the press and the public, publicized a considerable amount of classified material, and successfully defused the explosive "MacArthur issue." Such detached opinion as there was concluded that the hero had been a troublesome one and that the harassed President had done about what he had to do.

The Senate Hearings

The manner, form, and rules of the hearings set a record for Senate ambivalence. They were conducted in secret, but the stenographic transcript was made public every evening. However, before its release Admiral Arthur C. Davis, acting for the Pentagon, censored those parts whose publication he considered prejudicial to national defense. His censoring was not severe.

The combined committees had a membership of twenty-six senators, each of whom in order of seniority had an equal right to question each witness. In order to give themselves equal access to publicity the senators voted to restrict questioning to a short period at bat with as many turns as necessary to satisfy the members. This gave a witness with some adroitness the opportunity to deprive the questioning of much continuity and penetration, since he could talk as long as he wanted in answering each question, thus putting off searching follow-up until the next time around, which the senator might miss.

My testimony before the committees may conservatively be described as extensive. It began on Friday morning, June 1, 1951, at 10:06 and continued all day every day except Sunday until Saturday afternoon, June 9 at 5:05. Before recessing, Senator Russell observed dryly:

Mr. Secretary, I do not know whether it would be the source of pride or consolation to you, but your examination here has been the most extensive of any witness who has been before a hearing that has become somewhat noted for the thoroughness not to mention the repetition of the examination.

You have far exceeded in the number of questions, the number of words and the number of hours that you have been upon the stand the record of any previous witness.[1]

Then with some kind words of appreciation he released me.

Early in the questioning the senators began touching on our postwar relations with China. It was clear to me that a hash would be made of this complex matter if it was covered only by hit-or-miss questions and answers in the interstices of examinations that wandered from my qualifications to discuss military operations with the Chiefs of Staff to the admission of German scientists into the United States to the problems of oil companies in Iran and on to the loyalty program in the Department of State. I asked and obtained permission to postpone questions on China until Monday, when I would make a complete statement on the subject, after which I would be happy to be cross-examined. Adrian Fisher alerted the Far Eastern Bureau to collect for me the principal documents, arranged in chronological order, which I would take to the country for study through Saturday night and Sunday, unbothered by people or suggestions.

For weary hours, aided by coffee and a farmhouse policed into silence by my wife, with a security officer at the gate, I culled out the most telling documents and made a pile of rough notes. On Monday morning, June 4, at 10:03, tired but loaded, I heard Senator Russell launch my effort:

The committees will be in order.

Upon motion made and passed at the last sitting of the committees, the Secretary of State was to make a statement to the committees this morning on China policy.

Mr. Secretary, you may proceed in your own way.

The statement [2] occupied most of the morning and went off surprisingly well. For the first time it put together in colloquial, popular form an account of the century-long disintegration of China's ancient institutions and ways of life from collision with the Western world. To this I added as frankly as I could the reasons for the failure of our effort to aid in reconciling the two Chinese attempts at creating a modern and united China—the Nationalist effort and the Communist effort—a reconciliation they both professed to want. Most of this was new and perplexing to the senators; they never quite regained the initiative in dealing with it or me. Senator Alexander Wiley, the first to question me after the state-

1. *Hearings on the Military Situation in the Far East*, p. 2290.
2. *Ibid.*, pp. 1837–57.

ment, voiced this perplexity: "I think you should be complimented on a pretty clear-cut statement as to the facts that heretofore were not brought to our attention in relation to this Chinese situation, and a very clear-cut statement of the complex position that we occupied in seeking to find the way to combat the Communist influence." [3] Perhaps the most plaintive, if somewhat naïve, cry of "Foul!" came from Senator Owen Brewster, Republican of Maine, who complained that I had an "unfair advantage" over the senators through greater knowledge of the subject matter. The Senator had what Senator Wiley might have called a "clear-cut" point.

Senator Russell piloted the two committees into safe haven with great skill and wise judgment. Aware that any reference to the committees' terms of reference would only open partisan rifts and bickering, he treated those terms with intelligent neglect. Instead of a majority report, which would have invited a minority report, he dealt with those gloriously broad generalities to which the wise and just could repair, thus turning the committees from unhappy differences to universal agreement. "The issues which might divide our people," he told our friends and enemies alike, "are far transcended by the things which unite them. If threatened danger becomes war, the aggressor would find at one stroke arrayed against him the united energies, the united resources, and the united devotion of all the American people." [4] This is the sort of political management at which "leaders" in the Senate become past masters. If it does not heal old wounds, it does not inflict new ones. It records that the virulent period of a political virus has passed.

Reflections

As one looks back in calmness, it seems impossible to overestimate the damage that General MacArthur's willful insubordination and incredibly bad judgment did to the United States in the world and to the Truman Administration in the United States. During the Senate hearings a good deal of discussion revolved about whether the General had disobeyed orders in a court-martial sense of the phrase. I believe that he probably did not and that the debate is beside the point. The General was surely bright enough to understand what his Government wanted him to do. General Ridgway, who succeeded him, understood perfectly and achieved the desired ends. MacArthur disagreed with the desired ends, and wished instead to unify Korea by force of arms even though this

3. *Ibid.*, p. 1858.
4. *Ibid.*, p. 3125.

plan would involve general war with China and, quite possibly, with the Soviet Union as well. Indeed, far from being dismayed by this prospect, he seemed, as his letter to Congressman Martin strongly suggests, to welcome the wider war, for it was in Asia, as he saw it, that "the Communist conspirators [i.e., the Soviet Union and China] have elected to make their play for global conquest, and that we [i.e., he] have joined the issue thus raised on the battle-field." [5] Having joined the issue thus raised on the Asian battlefield, he was willing, not to say eager, to fight it out there. This was exactly what his Government had told him, beginning with the directive of September 27 and continuing until his relief, that it would not do, even if to avoid it involved withdrawal from Korea. Nevertheless he pressed his will and his luck to a shattering defeat.

In appraising its consequences, two conclusions stand out: the defeat with its losses of men and national prestige was quite avoidable had he followed the agreed plan of campaign; the defeat and MacArthur's conduct in defeat profoundly changed both the national attitude toward the war and our allies' confidence in the judgment and leadership of the United States Government and, especially, in its control over General MacArthur. Regarding the first conclusion, we have already noted that when General Ridgway took over command of the Eighth Army and later the supreme command, he was able, starting much farther south, after a defeat and opposed by a strong enemy, to stabilize the front as MacArthur had been told to do and to hold it. Had General MacArthur, who faced no opposition after Inchon and the defeat of the North Koreans, occupied one of the strong positions in mid-Korea, fortified it, and kept his forces collected, he could have shattered a Chinese assault just as Ridgway did.

The effects of defeat and the General's ill-concealed disaffection upon domestic and foreign confidence were equally plain. The enthusiasm with which our people and allies received President Truman's bold leadership of the United Nations in military resistance to aggression survived even the hard fighting of the retreat to the Pusan perimeter and the surprising discovery of North Korean military competence and toughness. It was heightened by the September victories and the complete collapse of the invasion of South Korea. Opinion at home and abroad would have remained steady and united had the Army under the September 27 plan and directive sealed off the South from further attack until the war should peter out, as it eventually did, even though this would re-

5. *Ibid.*, p. 3544.

quire, as it also did, some hard fighting to prove the strength of the line.

What lost the confidence of our allies were MacArthur's costly defeat, his open advocacy of widening the war at what they rightly regarded as unacceptable risks, and the hesitance of the Administration in asserting firm control over him. What disturbed and divided our own people was the stream of propaganda flowing out of Tokyo that the cause of MacArthur's disasters was not his own stubborn folly, but conspiracy in Washington, probably inspired by concern for national interests other than our own. The method and source of propaganda are well illustrated by a 1956 effusion of MacArthur's Chief of Staff, General Courtney Whitney: "Who it was who won over President Truman's confidence and corrupted his logic to the extent of defying the experienced advice of his best military experts, has always been a well-kept Washington secret. Certainly the Secretary of Defense, Louis Johnson, did not favor this kind of appeasement. So the likely person to bear the enormous blame for this incalculable mistake would seem to be the then Secretary of State Dean Acheson, possibly acting under pressure from the British Foreign Office." [6]

Nor does this apt pupil of Joseph McCarthy spare the President. Whitney states that MacArthur's "qualified guess" given the President at Wake Island, which deprecated the possibility of Chinese intervention, was based on the assumption that intervention would result in forceful retaliation, not continued sanctuary. Someone must have told the Chinese that they could intervene with impunity. The Wake Island conference, he concludes, was "a sly political ambush" set by the President for the General.

That General Whitney included all persons in high office in the plot against his hero is clear in his exculpation of the General for his sabotage of the President's intended statement before our forces crossed the 38th parallel for the second time: "What had happened was that by sheer accident, in his statement [of March 24, 1951] and in its reference to settling the war without reference to Formosa or the United Nations seat, MacArthur had cut right across one of the most disgraceful plots in American history. Or was it not accident, but intuition? This I do know: had MacArthur fully realized the hornets' nest he would stir up, he still would not have been deterred." [7] The last sentence I am inclined to believe. The continued seepage of this poison, like that administered by McCarthy, had a highly toxic effect on the American public. Like

6. Whitney, *MacArthur: His Rendezvous with History*, pp. 370–71.
7. *Ibid.*, p. 468.

McCarthy's, it was skillfully used by the Republican right and had an effect in undermining confidence in the very institution of government in areas far wider than those where such slanderous nonsense was believed. Like air pollution, one did not have to believe in it to be poisoned by it.

This loss of confidence at home and abroad in the conduct of our foreign affairs was not the proximate cause of any change in our foreign policy, but it added to our difficulties and by so doing diminished our effectiveness. The loss of support in the United Nations and the increased energy spent on countering unwise proposals we shall see as one manifestation of this. Another was to be growing opposition in other parts of the world to the policies and interests of the United States. This flame of opposition was skillfully and strongly fanned by the Soviet Union in 1951.

VII

THE MOVE FOR AN ARMISTICE

AT THE TIME OF General MacArthur's relief and General Ridgway's succession to Supreme Command, the UN forces were dug in on the Kansas line with a Chinese offensive ominously building up. To prepare for this, General Ridgway pushed a salient forward in the center of his line toward first the Utah and then the Wyoming line. The offensive burst with great fury ten days after General MacArthur's relief and continued for a month, checked in midcourse by General Van Fleet's counterattack.

For two weeks the Eighth Army gave ground as successive collapses of South Korean units under pressure opened gaps in the line. None of these, however, was permitted to develop into a breakthrough. As it fell back across the 38th parallel the Army traded ground for terrific losses inflicted on the enemy. When the first Chinese effort was spent, General Ridgway resumed the offensive, straightened his line on ground that he had strongly prepared, and sternly forbade his forces to be separated or strung out in pursuit. The Chinese resumed their attack in mid-May, but by the end of the month, after heavy losses, were in flight north of the parallel. The Eighth Army followed collectedly, soon had South Korea cleared of the enemy, and, resuming its position on the Kansas line, felt out the enemy's forces dug into strong positions farther north.

During early June, the White House, the State Department, the Pentagon, and the Supreme Command in Tokyo found themselves united on political objectives, strategy, and tactics for the first time since the war had started. The political purpose was to

stop the aggression and to leave the unification of Korea to time
and political measures. The strategy was to fight it out on the
Kansas-Wyoming line and at the Punch Bowl just north of it if it
took all summer, or more than two summers; our tactics were to
lure the enemy into assaults on strongly fortified lines through prepared and calibrated fields of fire. Experience had taught a costly
lesson: to push the Chinese back upon their border—their source
of reinforcement and supply—only increased their strength, as Her-
cules increased that of Antaeus when he threw him upon his Mother
Earth, while decreasing our own as our forces attenuated their lines
of supply, became separated, and lost touch with their air support
as they moved north. The generals, among them James Van Fleet
and Mark Clark, who later declared that they had been deprived
of their chance for total victory were antedating thoughts conceived
in tranquility.[1]

    While General Ridgway was pushing the Communists north,
I had an opportunity to drive home before the Congress and the
public the difference between the war aims of the United Nations
Command and the long-range United Nations political purposes
first stated in 1947 and since reiterated in the resolutions of October
7, 1950, and May 18, 1951. They had become confused by General

1. See, for example, Ridgway, *The Korean War*, p. 181.

June 1, 1951. A special sort of limelight. The author at the Senate
investigation into the dismissal of General MacArthur. Seated at left are
Republican Senators William F. Knowland and Harry P. Cain. ACME PHOTO

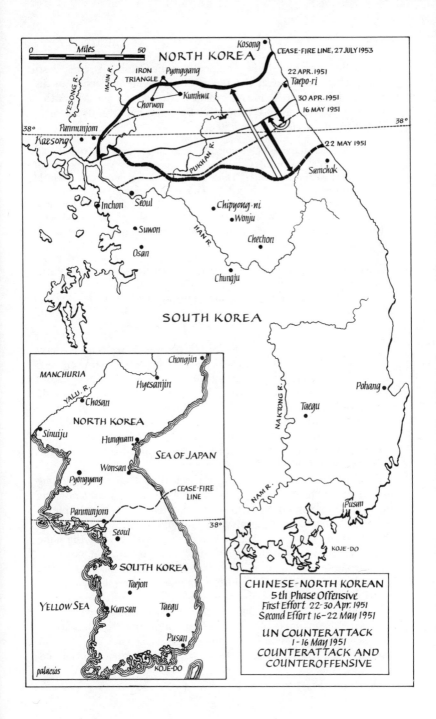

CHINESE-NORTH KOREAN
5th Phase Offensive
First Effort 22-30 Apr. 1951
Second Effort 16-22 May 1951

UN COUNTERATTACK
1-16 May 1951
COUNTERATTACK AND
COUNTEROFFENSIVE

MacArthur's oratory during the period from October 1950 to April 1951, when the General was repeatedly speaking and acting in disregard of President Truman's orders. Twice during the MacArthur hearings on June 1 and 2, 1951, I took the opportunity to make this distinction clear beyond doubt.[2]

SECRETARY ACHESON: Our objective is to stop the attack, end the aggression on that [Korean] Government, restore peace, providing against the renewal of the aggression. Those are the military purposes for which, as we understand it, the United Nations troops are fighting.

The United Nations has since 1947 and the United States has since 1943 or 1944 [the Cairo Declaration of December 1, 1943] stood for a unified, free, and democratic Korea. That is still our purpose, and is still the purpose of the United Nations.

I do not understand it to be a war aim. In other words, that is not sought to be achieved by fighting, but it is sought to be achieved by peaceful means, just as was being attempted before this aggression.

CHAIRMAN CONNALLY: After the fight—by peaceful means after the fighting is over.

SECRETARY ACHESON: Yes, sir.

The next morning Senator Smith of New Jersey took me over the same ground and asked specifically whether my answers suggested "the possibility of a cease-fire at or near the thirty-eighth parallel?" I replied: "If you could have a real settlement, that would accomplish the military purposes in Korea. That is if the aggression would end and you had reliable assurances that it would not be resumed, then you could return to a peacetime status, and we would hope gradually to remove the troops from Korea, both Chinese troops and United Nations troops."

While the diplomatic front in the United Nations and among our allies was relatively calm, we could not count on its remaining so. On May 18 months of effort had resulted in a UN vote for an embargo against sending strategically important items to China and North Korea. But a vote and an actual embargo were not the same thing; plenty of opportunity remained for congressional sanctions against nations that continued to export. We remembered, too, the anguish caused by the UN First Committee's Five Principles for Discussion of January 13, 1951, which we in the State Department thought it best to accept and which our fellow citizens rejected in no uncertain manner. Not being eager for further UN initiatives, it was incumbent upon us to devise our own. The only hopeful path pointed toward an armistice which might harden into an end

2. *Hearings on the Military Situation in the Far East*, pp. 1729–30, 1782.

to belligerency. An agreed settlement seemed both impossible and unreliable if achieved. One conclusion we shared unanimously: that exploration through the public procedures of the United Nations or through leaky foreign offices like the Indian would be fatal.

Peace Feelers

We therefore cast about like a pack of hounds searching for a scent. First Charles Bohlen, who was then in Paris at the Palais Rose, sounded out Vladimir Semyenov, Political Adviser to the Chairman of the Soviet Control Commission in Germany, without result. Then Ernest Gross and Thomas Cory at the United Nations got a faint scent from some informal words spoken by either Malik or Semen K. Tsarapkin, the alternate Soviet UN Representative, or both. The prompt appearance of a similar rumor in *The New York Times* drew protests and denials from the Russians, during which the scent died away. That channel proved to be too amateur. A suggestion with some credentials of reliability came to us that an approach to Peking might be more productive. We tried it secretly through both American and Swedish channels to Moscow without result. Charles Burton Marshall of the Policy Planning Staff went to Hong Kong and made himself available for contacts, but with no success. A last effort, however, initiated with the President's approval, produced results, not all of them foreseen.

The Kennan-Malik Talks

Our colleague George Kennan was on leave of absence from the Department working at the Institute for Advanced Study in Princeton. Remembering Philip Jessup's success with Malik over the Berlin blockade in 1949, Deputy Under Secretary H. Freeman Matthews asked Kennan to Washington in mid-May 1951 to talk with him and me. We wanted him to see Malik. Kennan was not a part of but was close to the official establishment and deeply interested in U.S.-Soviet relations (on which, in fact, he was then writing a history). They could talk seriously but without commitment. Our two countries seemed to be headed for what could be a most dangerous collision over Korea. This was definitely not the purpose of American actions or policy. It was hard for us to believe that it was desired by the Soviet Union. Whether or not it was desired by Peking, it seemed the inevitable result of the course the Chinese were steering. If the drift to serious trouble was to be stopped, the method would seem to be an armistice and cease-fire in Korea at about where the forces were. We would like to know how Moscow viewed the situation, and what, if any, suggestions it might have. We also wished to be sure that it understood our desires and intentions. If hostilities were to end, it was a good time to set about ending them.

We did not want George to negotiate anything, but to make sure that our purposes and intentions were absolutely clear to the Russians and that they were realistically aware of the course on which all were adrift and of its more than likely terminus. He agreed to take on the mission in his own way and alone. Through the Chiefs of Staff we let Ridgway know that an operation was on and that he should be prepared to advise on all relevant military matters and to conduct proceedings in the field as needed. He welcomed the development.

George, in a longhand note delivered by a young assistant in our UN delegation to Malik at his apartment in New York, asked to see him and for a reply by phone to Princeton. A prompt reply invited him to Malik's summer house on Long Island. Kennan drove from Princeton. They met quite alone on May 31 and spoke in Russian. Overcoming an initial embarrassment when Malik upset a tray of fruit and wine on himself, they circuitously approached the question, which, predictably, Malik was unable to answer, and as circuitously retreated from it, agreeing to meet again when he had had a chance to consider the matter, a euphemism for consulting Moscow. The next week, when they met again on June 5, Malik was able to tell him that the Soviet Government wanted peace and a peaceful solution in Korea and as rapidly as possible. It could not appropriately take part in discussions of a cease-fire. Malik's personal advice was to approach the North Koreans and Chinese. No doubt existed in any of our minds that the message was authentic. It had, however, a sibylline quality which left us wondering what portended and what we should do next.

Clarification began soon afterward, when on June 23 Malik delivered a speech on the UN radio program. The Soviet peoples believed, he said, that the conflict in Korea could be settled: "[A]s a first step discussions should be started between the belligerents for a cease-fire and an armistice providing for the mutual withdrawal of forces from the 38th parallel." [3] Could such a step be taken? he asked, and answered that it could if both sides really wished to to stop the fighting. This sounded as official as it was possible to be, but doubts were expressed at home and abroad, publicly and privately. Inquiry made through Ambassador Kirk in Mos-

3. *Department of State Bulletin*, Vol. XXV, July 9, 1951, p. 45, footnote 1.

cow confirmed that the views expressed were those of the Soviet Government and that Gromyko was uninformed about those of the Chinese.

The Decision to Negotiate Through Ridgway

The ambassadors of the nations with forces in the UN Command met and approved the opening of negotiations. The question was how. The case for military talks through commanders in the field was strong, for the following reasons:

First, because neither the Chinese nor the North Korean authorities were official entities recognized by the United States.

Second, because it was highly desirable to exclude from the talks political questions such as Formosa, the recognition of Communist China and its membership in the United Nations, and Indochina, which the Communists had tried to introduce earlier.

Third, because General Wu Hsiu-chuan's visit to the United Nations in New York to represent China there left no doubt that the UN was the worst of all places to conduct discussions.

Fourth, because the very fact that negotiations were in prospect was dictated by the relation of forces on the battlefield.

Fifth, because neither the Chinese Communists nor the Soviet Government accepted any responsibility for Chinese forces in Korea. They were supposed to be "volunteers," acting on their own responsibility. However, their commander could speak for them, as Gromyko pointed out to Ambassador Kirk.

Strong, however, as were the arguments for military conduct of discussions at the front, the military did not grasp for this responsibility; on the contrary, they were most reluctant to be tagged with it. When the President decided they should handle it, however, they loyally accepted the assignment.[4] Two basic papers were prepared in accordance with President Truman's orderly procedures: a small State-Defense group at Assistant Secretary-flag rank drafted a message covering Ridgway's opening of contact with the enemy and instructions, to be supplemented later, regarding the purposes, content, and conduct of the talks. These were gone over and revised by the Chiefs of Staff, General Marshall, General Ridgway, and me; submitted to the President; and, after incorporation of his changes, signed and dispatched. We also kept Ambassador

4. All the services shared in the task. The negotiating team consisted of Vice Admiral C. Turner Joy, U.S. Navy, chief delegate; Major General Paik Sun Yup, Republic of Korea Army; Major General Laurence C. Craigie, U.S. Air Force; Major General Henry I. Hodes, U.S. Eighth Army; and Rear Admiral Arleigh A. Burke, U.S. Navy.

Muccio informed and later, through him, President Syngman Rhee. I myself saw that Senators Tom Connally and Alexander Wiley and Representatives James Richards and Charles Eaton were abreast of developments. Muccio soon warned us that we were in for trouble with Rhee, as indeed we were. What Muccio called "his mania for reunification" would and did lead him to regard as "unacceptable" (a word of the old diplomatic vocabulary denoting a cause for restrained fury) any cessation of our fighting for the reunification of Korea. Some rather plain telegrams restored better behavior but did not gain real acceptance of the policy.

On June 30, Toyko time, General Ridgway broadcast to the Commander in Chief, Communist Forces in Korea, that if, as reported, the Communist commander was prepared to negotiate a cease-fire and armistice, Ridgway was prepared to send a representative to begin discussions. How different this simple, soldierly, and disciplined announcement was from the unauthorized bombast by which General MacArthur frustrated President Truman's proposed announcement of a similar sort three months before—not that an earlier one, if it had been made, would have produced a useful response. General Ridgway's six months of hard fighting and the terrible punishment he had inflicted upon the enemy had drastically changed the situation. Furthermore, his conduct had restored respect for the governmental integrity of the United States.

Foul-up as Negotiations Start

On July 2 the Communist commanders replied favorably to General Ridgway's message. Whereas he had suggested meeting on a Danish hospital ship in Wonsan harbor, they proposed Kaesong, a town at that time between the two lines. General Ridgway accepted the change and the delegations met on July 10. Almost at once we learned the truth of Bret Harte's observation a century before:

> That for ways that are dark
> And for tricks that are vain,
> The heathen Chinee is peculiar.[5]

Whereas Kaesong had been between the lines when General Ridgway agreed to it as the seat of discussions, by the time discussions began the Communists had surrounded it and proceeded to make an arrogant and offensive propaganda demonstration, excluding the allied press and behaving in their customary ill-mannered and

---

5. Francis Bret Harte, "Plain Language from Truthful James."

boorish way. Whereupon we broke off contact until they restored the neutral aspect of the meeting place.

Then we ran into the now familiar trouble of agreement on the agenda items. The first two substantive items on the Chinese agenda caused the trouble. The first of these was "establishment of the 38th Parallel as the military demarcation line between the two sides and establishment of a demilitarized zone, as basic conditions for the cessation of hostilities in Korea"; the second was "withdrawal of all armed forces of foreign countries from Korea." [6] We could not accept either. The 38th parallel had been amply proved to be indefensible and to us had no political or historic significance. We had no intention of giving up the strong positions of the Kansas line; indeed, we hoped to improve them. The second item had been familiar Communist propaganda for months in regard to both Asia and Europe. Their aim, of course, was to push American forces back to North America.

Expecting months of verbal quibbling on these items, as there had been at the Palais Rose, General Marshall and I both made public statements. President Rhee, as I have said, was most disturbed by the armistice discussions. We doubted whether his morale could withstand a long propaganda battle at Kaesong directed at leaving the South Korean Army without allies after an armistice on an indefensible line. I spoke on July 19 and General Marshall on the twenty-fourth, strongly affirming that the removal of foreign troops was a political matter inappropriate for discussion by commanders arranging an armistice. A United Nations force must and would, we said, remain in Korea until peace was firmly established. This greatly comforted President Rhee, who thought, according to Muccio, that the "message was fine, very reassuring, just what we wanted." The Korean National Assembly also approved a message of gratitude. President Truman directed us to stick to this line, keeping in close touch with him.

To our great surprise, however, the Communists dropped the battle over the wording of the agenda. They rephrased the item on a military demarcation line and a demilitarized zone so as not to refer to any particular line, and dropped the withdrawal-of-forces item. But, as the talks moved to take up agenda topics, they made it plain that on the 38th parallel, at least, they had not at all changed their substantive position. The line of demarcation must still be the 38th parallel. With the agenda agreed in two weeks—

6. Walter G. Hermes, *Truce Tent and Fighting Front,* second volume published in *United States Army in the Korean War* (Washington, D.C.: Office of the Chief of Military History, U.S. Army, 1966), p. 24.

a phenomenal feat—we settled down to discuss it, happily unaware that final agreement would not be reached until two years later and that even agreement on the first item would take the next six months.

How and why did this happen? Were we deceived and led into an endless propaganda morass? To some degree. Was it due to a relaxation of military pressure on the enemy? Certainly not in 1951. Was it due to a change of mind by the Russians or a difference of view between them and the Chinese? To some extent, the latter. The reasons, I believe, were far more complex than many simplistic explanations given over the years. One, I think, unsuspected by me at the time, was of our own making and occurred at the very beginning.

Three years after these events some of us who had been deeply involved in their direction met from time to time to discuss old campaigns, as soldiers will, and analyze, with more time and detachment than the press of events had permitted, the reasons why we and others acted as we did. At one of these meetings several of my colleagues suggested that the Russians and Chinese could well have been surprised, chagrined, and given cause to feel tricked when at Kaesong we revealed a firm determination as a matter of major principle not to accept the 38th parallel as the armistice line. There were several reasons why they might have felt so. In the first place, when Kennan spoke to Malik, the Eighth Army had only recently crossed the 38th parallel; indeed, its western flank was south of it. While Kennan spoke only vaguely of a truce line, Malik in his radio address was very precise in referring to a "mutual withdrawal of forces from the 38th parallel." Furthermore, our initial agenda provided for "limitation of discussion to purely military matters related to Korea only," [7] and since the Japanese surrender we had insisted that the parallel was wholly a military line without political significance. To change it, therefore, might well have, in the Communists' minds, political significance. Even more important, and unknown to us either in 1945 when the parallel was chosen or in 1951, the 38th parallel had been a most important line to both Imperial Russia and Imperial Japan prior to the Russo-Japanese war and the annexation of Korea by Japan, for it was the line proposed by Japan but rejected by Russia as too restrictive as the demarcation of their spheres of influence in Korea.

So it seems to me highly probable that the Russians and the Chinese, for whom they were acting, received a considerable shock when at the start of a negotiation to restore, as they thought, the

7. *Ibid.*, p. 23.

status quo ante they found us demanding a new line for our sphere of influence, not only more militarily significant but involving considerable loss of prestige for them. They would never imagine that what appeared to be trickery was wholly inadvertent on our part. It was exactly the sort of maneuver in which they would have delighted.

Toward the end of July 1951 in response to a thoughtful letter from the British Secretary of State for Foreign Affairs, Herbert Morrison, I speculated on what might come out of these talks and their possible aftermath, allowing my mind to roam ahead. Chinese purposes, I thought, might be narrower and more immediate than Russian, with the former more concentrated on gaining control of the peninsula and the latter looking toward the longer-range purpose of slowing down or stopping the military defense of the West. But this difference would hardly benefit us. I thought that the prospects of "a general settlement in Korea" were not good, which was Morrison's view also. The Communists wished to eliminate our influence from Korea altogether; the MacArthur aim of unifying Korea by force entailed costs greater than we were prepared to pay. I would regard an armistice, therefore, as something that we must live with for a considerable time and that must be adapted to that end. On this issue we must expect trouble from Rhee, with his "mania for reunification"; he would oppose anything less and might try to prevent it. So I saw the best hope as not searching for an illusory general solution, but in aiming persistently toward an armistice that would stop the fighting in a posture favorable to the defense and, given the presence of UN troops over a considerable time, might harden into a maintainable peace. Morrison was gratified that we were thinking along the same lines. We must now wait and see what would develop, he said. And wait we did.

Negotiations Off and Fighting On

At Kaesong the discussion wore on repetitively about the demarcation line, interrupted from August 4 to 10 when armed Chinese forces violated the neutrality of the conference zone. Our negotiators, understandably frustrated by the endless and circuitous path they trod, urged that we give the Communists a limited time to choose between alternatives, and if they did not, that we break off negotiations. But we in Washington felt that being ahead so far we must put the onus for a break squarely on the other side. On August 20 brief hope dawned when the Communists seemed willing to consider the "line of contact" on the crucial date rather than "the general area of the battle line"—our phrase—as the armistice demarcation line. But before the significance of this phrase could be explored, the other side broke off negotiations, charging that an American plane had bombed and strafed Kaesong. The United Nations Command investigated and denied the charges. On September 6 General Ridgway proposed that talks be resumed at a new site, but four days later one of our planes did strafe the Kaesong conference site. Proper disciplinary action was taken, and the Communists, their *amour propre* satisfied, proposed resumption of negotiations but at Kaesong, not at a new site. This started a new procedural controversy.

Since the beginning of the second year of the war, negotiating and fighting had been going on together, the latter more successfully from our point of view. After a review of strategy by the commanders in the field, they rejected ideas of advancing to the neck of Korea along the Pyongyang-Wonsan line in favor of strengthening and shortening the Kansas line by taking over the enemy positions ringing the Punch Bowl. These were strong positions that enabled the Communists to enfilade the Kansas line. When, in early autumn after heavy fighting and severe casualties on both sides, Bloody Ridge had been taken, the Eighth Army made another assault to add a further strong point from which the enemy menaced its right flank. Appropriately named Heartbreak Ridge, it was in our hands by mid-October.

Negotiations Resumed at Panmunjom

A week or so later—possibly motivated by these successes of our arms—the Chinese accepted General Ridgway's proposal to resume negotiations at Panmunjom in a neutral and unoccupied zone. During the summer I put the Department to work devising courses to follow should the negotiations succeed and the fighting end, or should they fail and the enemy intensify his efforts. It seemed to me that inevitably and soon we should face one or the other of these contingencies; yet although we remained in office for another year and a half, we faced neither. The war neither stopped nor blazed up again in that time. It slumbered like an ominous and infinitely dangerous dragon, with no St. George at hand to slay it.

After the event both professional and armchair warriors have criticized the Government for not maintaining heavy offensive pressure on the enemy to speed up conclusion of the armistice. I am happy to say that the Supreme Commander took no such callous attitude toward the lives of his men, but, as General Ridgway himself has told us, did his best to keep our losses at a minimum and undertook no major offensives after perfecting his line.[8]

The Department's studies produced two works, known as the "optimistic paper" and the "pessimistic paper," the chief value of which was to assure us that no new ideas had been spawned since the days of the MacArthur crisis. They confirmed the views of all of us, soldiers and civilians alike, that we were on the only sound course and that we had to pull together to make it work. If still further confirmation were needed, we got it in September from the visits of Morrison and French Foreign Minister Robert Schuman and our talks with them.

Their enthusiasm for the Korean war had reached an irreducible minimum. The "optimistic paper," which looked forward to conferences for a settlement in Korea, seemed to them, as it did to us, beyond the realm of possibility. The "pessimistic paper" terrified them. Possible bombing of Chinese bases, blockades of China, trade embargoes, with the chances of Russian intervention in the Far or Middle East, proposals of expediting Japanese rearmament— all seemed as dangerous and undesirable to them as they did to us. We, however, were closer to the need for new fields of action. From the British side came the familiar exegesis on the perils to Hong Kong and the dangers of driving the Chinese into the arms of the Russians or vice versa. I often regretted that no embracing arms seemed ready to receive the United States if pushed too far.

8. Ridgway, *The Korean War*, pp. 182–83.

VIII

CRISIS OVER PRISONERS
OF WAR

EARLY IN 1952, a first-class crisis built up in Korea and burst upon General Ridgway just as he had been ordered to turn over the Far Eastern Command to General Mark Clark and take over General Eisenhower's command in Europe. As we have seen, in the last quarter of 1951 military action in Korea tapered off, reducing casualties progressively and drastically. General Ridgway took advantage of the lull to clean up the troublesome jetsam of the Communist retreat which had been left in the rear of the Eighth Army. By January 1952 nineteen thousand stragglers and guerrillas were killed or rounded up and the problem pretty well solved.

As the year began, General Ridgway was dug in on the Kansas line largely north of the parallel, the enemy facing him in an equally strong position. The armistice talks had stalled after agreement on the battle line of November 27, 1951, as the armistice line should an armistice be concluded within a month, which did not occur. The fallback arrangement then came into effect, which provided that the battle line on the date of the armistice, whatever and whenever that might be, would be the demarcation line. General Ridgway quotes with approval General Clark's summary of the military situation: " 'We never had enough men [to clear the Chinese out of Korea], whereas the enemy had sufficient manpower not only to block our offensives, but to make and hold small gains of his own. To have pushed it to a successful conclusion would have required more trained divisions and more supporting air and naval forces, would have incurred heavy casualties, and would have necessitated lifting our self-imposed ban on attacks on the enemy sanctuary north of the Yalu.' "

To this statement General Ridgway has added that "lifting that ban would have laid Japan open to attack and, if that had happened, would have greatly and immediately widened the war. No responsible leader in the United States at that time could have sold such a course to the American public." [1] Or, I might add, desired to do so. Furthermore, statements made in the press in recent years that commanders in the field (Van Fleet has been mentioned) urged heavy offensives only to be turned down in Washington are not true. The field and home commands were united on political and military policy.

The charge has been made that the military strategy carried out by Generals Ridgway and Clark of maintaining a strong defensive position by active tactical operations prolonged the war and greatly increased the casualties over the prior offensive period. That it prolonged the war is a purely argumentative assertion unsupported by any responsible military opinion of the period. There was no sensible alternative. Regarding casualties, however, the charge is provably erroneous. The Korean war was fought for a month and two days over three years. Armistice discussions began at the end of the first year—the year of the longest continued heavy fighting—and continued, off and on, for two years. United States casualty figures—which are the only accurate ones—were as follows:

	JUNE 1950–JUNE 1951 (inclusive)	JULY 1951–JULY 1953 (inclusive)
KILLED	21,300	12,300
WOUNDED	53,100	50,200
MISSING OR CAPTURED	4,400	700
Total	78,800	63,200

Thus the total figures for the next two years were less than for the first year alone. More than one-quarter of the casualties occurred during the last two months of the war, when the Communists put on two heavy offensives to try to get better terms from President Eisenhower than President Truman would give them. Their own losses for these two months have been calculated at 108,458. In the end the terms were exactly the same.[2]

1. Ridgway, *The Korean War*, pp. 203–4.
2. Casualty figures supplied by Walter G. Hermes, Office of Military History, U.S. Army; see Hermes, *Truce Tent and Fighting Front*, p. 477.

Voluntary Repatriation of Prisoners

The prisoners of war whom our forces had captured in Korea presented two problems of which we were aware and one that took us by surprise. The first was where to put so many prisoners—as many as 170,000 at one point—in a country where it was not possible to get very far from the battlefront. The second was determining the composition of the mass. How many of the prisoners were Chinese and what kind of Chinese—Communists or captured and impressed Nationalists? How many were North Koreans and collaborating South Koreans or captured and impressed southerners, soldiers and civilians? The third problem was a plot, early put into preparation by the enemy, to stir up revolt among this, to them, expendable mass to the propaganda disadvantage of the United States.

The first problem was thought solved by putting the prisoners in cantonments on the small and wholly inadequate island of Koje-do, just south of Pusan, where they soon became greatly overcrowded and got out of the control of the small and largely incompetent personnel detailed for the unpromising and disagreeable duty. The enemy resolved their problem by reducing their prisoner list from 65,000 to 11,559 by means of prisoners allegedly "released at the front" and re-enlisted in the North Korean forces, like the mass conversions practiced by the knights of the Teutonic Order in the fourteenth century. The task of classification began in deceptive calmness. Thirty-seven thousand were found to be South Koreans and were later released. In the process of screening, however, both sides became aware of broader problems. On our side, we saw ourselves confronted again with the horrors encountered in Europe in 1945 when large numbers of Soviet civilians and Soviet soldiers who had deserted to the Germans and been recaptured by the allies committed suicide as they were being forcibly repatriated. The Communists on their side were determined never to open wide the invitation to desertion and escape that voluntary repatriation presented.

Not only did the matter precipitate a deep issue between the two sides, but also one between the State and Defense departments. The military were, understandably enough, primarily concerned with getting back their own men (a much smaller number) at the end of the fighting. They had been properly interested in separating out of the prisoner pens those of our own Korean allies who had been swept up in the confusion of war. But to insure the return of our enemy-held prisoners, the Pentagon favored the return of North Korean and Chinese prisoners and civilian internees regardless of their wishes. While no final position was taken within our government for several months, Admiral Ruthven E. Libby was instructed to put forward a proposal at Panmunjom on January 2, 1952, by which all prisoners should be released under equitable terms providing for voluntary repatriation as determined by an impartial organ such as the International Committee of the Red Cross. South Korean soldiers and civilians captured, whether or not incorporated in the North Korean armies, should be released and allowed to return home.

The proposal was immediately rejected and a violent propaganda war launched, enhanced by lurid Communist charges of germ warfare practices employed by the Americans against North Korea and China. The debate in Washington went through several stages. My colleagues and I were moved by humanitarian reasons and by the effect upon our own Asian peoples of the forcible repatriation of prisoners whose lives would be jeopardized. We were also aware of the deterrent effect upon the Communists of the escape offered to their soldiers by falling into our hands.

When our military colleagues argued that the Communists would never agree to voluntary repatriation, thus blocking an armistice, which we both believed to be in our interest, we suggested following the example of our enemies. This would mean finding out which prisoners would forcibly resist repatriation, releasing them at some appropriate time and then offering to exchange the rest. Even then a serious problem would remain—what to do with the non-Koreans who refused repatriation. In the meantime our proposal lent another argument to the urgent need for a screening and classification of the prisoners. At this point Senator William E. Jenner of Indiana, who had been contemplating a Senate resolution on this complex subject, was dissuaded by the invaluable efforts of Secretary of Defense Lovett and a group of senators from hopelessly prejudicing General Ridgway's negotiations.

At the end of February a series of meetings with the President, in which the top civilian officers of Defense did not oppose State, resulted in his decision that the United States would not and could not agree to forcible repatriation. Thus we took our basic position, from which we never afterward wavered. The execution of the decision did not proceed as planned. Circumstances unforeseen and embarrassing intruded.

At this stage in the negotiations at Panmunjom we were hopeful that only three major obstacles stood in the way of concluding an armistice. The fighting had died down; it was agreed that the armistice line should be drawn at about that held by the forces when the armistice was signed; and a good many other arrangements had been worked out. The prisoner-of-war issue, our insistence that airfields in North Korea not be repaired or new ones constructed, and the composition of the armistice-supervising commission remained. Our plan, developed by mid-March, was to screen the prisoners and to trade off the first two issues—voluntary repatriation to be accepted by them and repair of airfields by us. The two sides were theoretically agreed on an impartial commission, but by impartial they meant noncombatant—specifically, they wanted the Soviet Union a member—while we meant neutral. One solution for this was to have a really neutral commission or, if they chose, a really bipartisan one with both the United States and the USSR and some real neutral like the Swiss. General Ridgway, fearing retaliation against our captive men, preferred to continue the effort for agreed screening. In the course of this our negotiators made an unfortunate guess, communicated to the other side, that 116,000 of the 130,000 or more prisoners held by the UN Command would be repatriated. Early in April the Communists agreed to screening by both sides. We seemed to be making progress.

By mid-April a disconcerting report came in from General Ridgway. At the time of the movement to Koje-do, prisoners of South Korean origin were separated from North Koreans. This produced camps predominantly and violently (but not unanimously) anti-Communist and pro-Communist. In February trouble between South Korean guards and internees in a civilian compound had begun over screening, resulting in seventy-seven prisoner fatalities. Again in March twelve prisoners were killed. General Ridgway now reported that 37,000 prisoners in seven of the seventeen compounds could not be screened without the use of force. The Communists reported 12,000 prisoners—7,900 Korean, 4,100 non-Korean—willing to return. It was a rough estimate, then, that the UN Command gave: 70,000 could be repatriated without force —5,100 Chinese and 64,900 Koreans. The rest could not be.

Revolt in the Compounds

When our figures were reported to the Communists, they were greeted by violent and angry outbursts, charges of bad faith, refusal of neutral screening, and increased disorder in the compounds. It had become clear that this disorder was directly controlled from Panmunjom by messengers surrendering to our forces for the purpose of bringing orders and by concerted action arranged through conferences in the prisoners' hospitals and by other means. On May 7, the day before open plenary sessions were resumed at Panmunjom with the prisoner issue now the outstanding one left, Brigadier General Francis T. Dodd, inadequately attended, entered POW Camp No. 1 to negotiate with the prisoners and was himself taken prisoner and held as hostage for the satisfaction of their demands. After the earlier riots and again on May 5, General Ridgway had ordered, without results, that discipline be restored in the camps. He was due to leave within the week for his NATO command, where I was to meet him in three weeks' time.

Faced with this new insurgency, Ridgway ordered that the camps be entered immediately and discipline restored. Although forces were assembled, no action was taken. General Dodd was released on the eleventh after his successor, Brigadier General Charles F. Colson, had accepted the humiliating terms negotiated by Dodd. General Mark Clark promptly repudiated the agreement, relieved both Dodd and Colson with recommendation that they be demoted, and renewed General Ridgway's orders. On June 10 our troops entered the camps and, after a pitched battle in which thirty-one prisoners and one American soldier were killed, began the re-establishment of control. The prisoners were redivided, separating the pro-Communist and anti-Communist and ending the overcrowding by sending many to new camps elsewhere. With the exception of an attempted break-out in one camp in December, in which eighty-five were killed and a hundred hospitalized, trouble within the prisoner-of-war camps ended.

This bungled military operation in the field, like General MacArthur's disastrous advance to the Yalu, shook our allies' faith in the good judgment and competence of our command, creating doubt of our ability to furnish leadership in the great affairs where it had been entrusted to us. I felt this dubiety in May when I reached Europe. We had not yet restored order in the prisoners' camps and the fury of the propaganda campaign against us, to which we had so generously contributed, continued unabated. I was to feel it again in the autumn, when the return of the prisoners would become the principal question before the General Assembly.

Senator Richard Russell of Georgia, Chairman of the Armed Services Committee, suggested to the President that to reassure foreign opinion of the good faith of our conduct toward the prisoners a military commission from neutral nations—he mentioned India, Indonesia, and Pakistan—be asked to observe our treatment of the prisoners. The President approved, added Sweden and

Switzerland to the list, and asked Secretary Lovett to invite the inquiry. This was one of the very few instances when the President did not consult me on a matter of foreign policy. I heard of it over the radio and immediately warned him that the invitation would be declined. India and Indonesia backed away from the idea, and after a week or two it was permitted to fade out.

Before I went to Europe at the end of May, my colleagues in the Department, in discussions with their British associates, had come to believe that Chinese intentions about the prisoner issue might be profitably probed by the Indian Government through Ambassador Panikkar in Peking. To my mind the operation would be more likely to produce confusion from misinformation and imprecise ideas, but I agreed to speak to Eden about it. He favored it and our offices cooperated in the effort. As it came to nothing, no purpose would be served in following the labyrinthine course beyond noting an idea evolved by the Indians, which was to cause us trouble later in the autumn of 1952 during the maneuvering and negotiations at the General Assembly. This was to conclude an armistice on the basis of exchanging all the prisoners who would not forcibly resist repatriation and merely hold the rest for further negotiation. Both Defense and State rejected this nonsolution. It would, we believed, put a great strain on a fragile armistice and unconscionable pressure on the prisoners held in limbo.

When at the end of the summer private and public discussions of the prisoner issue had involved it in confusion and obscurity, the United Nations Command restated its proposal to cut through semantics and propaganda to reality. Three alternative proposals were put forward. Under the first, as soon as an armistice agreement went into effect all prisoners of war on either side would be entitled to release and repatriation. To give effect to this right they were to be brought in an orderly and manageable manner to an exchange point in the demilitarized zone and there identified and checked off against a list. Those not resisting repatriation were to be expeditiously exchanged. The others would be taken from the zone and released. Under the second, those who had indicated to the United Nations Command that they would forcibly resist repatriation would be entirely freed from military control of either side and interviewed by representatives of countries not participating in the Korean hostilities and freed to go to the side of their choice as then indicated. Under the third, nonrepatriates would be freed in the demilitarized zones to go where they chose.

Such was our position as we entered the session of the United Nations General Assembly beginning in mid-October 1952.

Bombing Bothers Britain

As already mentioned, fighting on the ground died down in 1952, with an occasional flare-up. Old Baldy was won in the summer and lost and won again in September. The Communist attack on White Horse Hill failed in October, as did ours at Snipers' Ridge and Triangle Hill. At year's end the stalemate continued. But enemy buildup was continuing, which Operation Strangle, an air campaign, had not at midyear been able to check. It was decided, therefore, within the Government to step up Operation Strangle.

At just this time Lord Alexander, Minister of Defense, and Selwyn Lloyd, Eden's deputy, were returning via Washington from a scouting mission to Korea. They had asked for a senior British officer on General Clark's staff to keep them better informed, to which we would agree, and a representative at Panmunjom, which we would refuse. While they were conferring with Secretary Lovett and General Bradley, the United Nations air and naval forces, in the largest combined air operations of the war, bombed power installations in North Korea on June 23 and 24, 1952. The largest plant hit was at Suiho on the Yalu, supplying both North Korea and Manchuria. Although this plant had been spared in prior bombing of power plants because it had been dismantled, it had been put back into operation and was supplying the Manchurian airfields. The attack on it, asked for by General Clark, had been widely cleared, including with me, and no objections had been interposed. A storm broke at once, and nowhere more violently than in London and in the Commons on June 24. Mr. Churchill and Mr. Eden, conceding that Britain had not been consulted, manfully defended the operation: power plants were legitimate military targets; there was good reason to attack them; they regretted that Her Majesty's Government had not been consulted but there was no obligation to do so. No one could ask more, but the House of Commons did.

I was in London at the time. Moreover, through the kindness of Mr. Eden I had been invited to address a group of members of all parties and both Houses of Parliament on June 26 in a large assembly room in Westminster Hall. Need I add that I had not planned it this way? At any rate, there was no need to worry about attendance, especially as I had agreed to respond to questions. The meeting was off the record, which gave me more latitude than would otherwise have been proper in a matter about which the Government and the opposition differed. Reports of what I said leaked out in garbled form and began to arouse some of my easily agitated critics in the Senate. To calm them the Department released the transcript on this subject:

If I may digress for a moment, I shall make some remarks about a matter which is one of controversy and which I would not speak about in England were it not for the fact that this is off-the-record. I shall restrict my remarks to what I think it is my duty to say to you at this time. This is about the matter that you have been debating in the last 2 or 3 days.

You would ask me, I am sure, if I did not say this, two questions, and I should like to reply very frankly to both of them. One question you would ask is: Shouldn't the British Government have been informed or consulted about this? To that, my answer would be "yes." It should have been; indeed, it was our intention to do it. It is only as the result of what in the United States is known as a "snafu" that you were not consulted about it.

I am sure that you are wholly inexperienced in England with government errors. We, unfortunately, have had more familiarity with them, and, due to the fact that one person was supposed to do something and thought another person was supposed to do [it], you were not consulted. . . . You should have been. We have no question about that.

If you ask me whether you had an absolute right to be consulted, I should say "no," but I don't want to argue about absolute right.

What I want to say is that you are a partner of ours in this operation, and we wanted to consult you; we should have, and we recognize an error.

Now you ask me whether this [i.e. the bombing] was a proper action. To that I say: Yes, a very proper action, an essential action. It was taken on military grounds. It was to bomb five plants, four of which were far removed from the frontier, one of which was on the frontier. We had not bombed these plants before because they had been dismantled, and we wished to preserve them in the event of unification of Korea. They had been put into operation once more; they were supplying most of the energy which was used not only by airfields which were operating against us but by radar which was directing fighters against our planes.[3]

My hearers seemed to approve. They applauded heartily when in reply to a question I said that the attack had been highly successful. Nevertheless, when I met privately with Eden, he pleaded for "no more surprises."

3. *Department of State Bulletin,* Vol. XXVII, July 14, 1952, p. 60.

IX

AN OPEN COVENANT
OPENLY CONNIVED AGAINST

For two months in the autumn of 1952 the General Assembly, meeting for the first time in its new headquarters in New York, sought a solution to the prisoner-of-war problem in Korea, which its members thought, quite erroneously, was holding up an armistice. The armistice was not to come until eight months later, after our election and bitter battles and heavy casualties in Korea had convinced the Communists that they could get no better terms than had already been proposed to them. From mid-October to early December I plunged more deeply than ever before into politics and diplomacy as practiced in the General Assembly, spending more time and playing a larger part in the new modernistic palace at Turtle Bay than I ever had done in the refurbished World's Fair building at Flushing Meadows or the sham and shoddy Palais de Chaillot.

The General Assembly, like all large international gatherings from Vienna to Versailles, had a public and a private side. In public, arguments were addressed to delegates only as they furnished a setting for broadcasts to world audiences, including, in this case, an American electorate engaged in a presidential campaign. So tricky did this last factor make the situation that both Eden and Schuman put off their arrival in New York until after the election of November 4. In private, leaders of various groups persuaded, exhorted, and intrigued to hold major allies together, to gain adherents for positions thought to affect negotiations at Panmunjom, or the will of belligerents, or—in some cases—merely to manipulate a large unwieldy, and confused body to some conclusion.

138   THE KOREAN WAR

My own purpose was to support armistice terms that our
Government, carrying the main responsibility for conducting the
war, believed would end the fighting with the greatest hope of
keeping it ended and of stability thereafter. To do this required
holding the British steadily on course with us, keeping the support
of the Latin American and European states, a group that could
defeat any harmful proposal and was essential to any useful one,
and, finally, guarding against proposals of two adroit operators,
Krishna Menon of India, leader of the Arab-Asian states, and Lester
B. Pearson of Canada, President of the Assembly. These would give
the appearance, without having the effect, of achieving our purpose,
thus gaining support among delegates from "uncommitted" nations.

The Central Issue and Its Ambiance

The central issue to occupy the seventh General Assembly
centered upon the return of prisoners of war. Our proposal for repatriation, without compulsion, of prisoners willing to return was
submitted to the other side on September 28, 1952, and categori-
cally rejected by them. Lieutenant General William K. Harrison,
who had succeeded Admiral Joy as our chief negotiator, suspended
further meetings until the other side had something to propose. At
my press conference on October 8 I supported this position, stress-
ing our willingness to resume discussion of old or new proposals but
not to compromise the humane principles we had enunciated. To
continue to put forward proposals in the face of adamant rejection
could soon amount to negotiating with oneself.

Usually "general debate" at the opening of General Assembly
annual meetings bored everyone and wasted time. However, in
1952, the time wasted in October was well spent, for although the
opening date had been delayed a month, the American election
was still three weeks off. General statements fairly innocuously dis-
posed of half this time. My own contribution to them, sober but
bland, is not worth recalling. By the last week in October even the
most ebullient orators at Turtle Bay had run dry and the beginning
of committee discussion could be put off no longer. The Korean
armistice was the first item on the agenda of the First Committee
and I was the first speaker. Debate opened on October 24.

In order to highlight discussion in the General Assembly we
prepared, and twenty nations [1] joined us in sponsoring, a resolution

1. The twenty nations joining the United States in sponsoring the resolution were
Australia, Belgium, Canada, Colombia, Denmark, Ethiopia, France, Greece, Hon-
duras, Iceland, Luxembourg, the Netherlands, New Zealand, Nicaragua, Norway, the
Philippines, Thailand, Turkey, the United Kingdom, and Uruguay.

that called upon the Chinese and North Koreans to "agree to an armistice which recognizes the rights of all prisoners of war to an unrestricted opportunity to be repatriated and avoids the use of force in their repatriation." Leading off in support of the resolution, I made a long speech.[2] There was no hurry, and to give the whole history of the Korean issue from its beginning in the Cairo Declaration of December 1, 1943, that Korea should be free and independent—a proposition accepted by the Soviet Union later—seemed to me the best way to answer all the falsehoods of Communist propaganda. Carefully documented and, to hold attention, made from notes rather than read, it took four hours to deliver. Afterward Sir Muhammad Zafrulla Khan, Foreign Minister of Pakistan and later Judge of the International Court of Justice, said to me, "I had no idea our case was so powerful."

We had hoped for quick action on the twenty-one-nation resolution, but it was not to be. The U.S. election was only eleven days away; my authenticity as a spokesman for the United States was at low ebb, for General Eisenhower's announcement that if elected he would go to Korea indicated that he was committing himself to nothing. My report to the President the day after the speech [3] shows me unduly optimistic:

Dear Mr. President:

After the first ten days of this session of the General Assembly, I think it is fair to report that things are moving for us perhaps better than we might have expected. This is, as you know, a tough session for us, because we are caught in the middle on most of the colonial issues, but we have done our best to make a virtue out of our predicament.

The organizational phase of this session has gone off more quietly and smoothly than usual. Partly, this reflects a gingerly feeling about our elections. And partly, this may be because the Russians have so far been operating under wraps. They have gone through a restrained rehash of their charges from previous years, but they have acted either with hesitancy or restraint. They have clearly not yet shown their full hand.

As we anticipated from our analysis of the Communist Party Congress in Moscow and related actions, the Russians are doing their best to isolate us from our allies, and to play upon all the differences in the non-Communist world. We have been interested to see how they would meet the dilemma of trying to woo the British and French away from us, and at the same time appeal to the people of the colonial areas. It looks as if they have decided to stress the latter, and let the former go for another time. They have lumped the British and French together with us as the Atlantic

2. For texts of the proposed resolution and excerpts from the speech, see *Department of State Bulletin*, Vol. XXVII, November 3, 1952, pp. 679–92, and November 10, 1952, pp. 744–51.

3. Letter from Secretary Acheson to President Truman, October 25, 1952.

warmongers, and have made strenuous appeals, both on the floor and in the lobbies, to the Arab-Asian bloc.

It appears to me that the outstanding political fact of the Assembly thus far has been the domination of the proceedings by the Arab-Asian group, which has been successful in every major effort up to this point. The Arab-Asian bloc has been exceptionally skillful in allying themselves with both the Latin Americans and Soviets on particular issues, obtaining majorities which could not be countered by votes of Western European and Commonwealth members. The solidity of this Arab-Asian bloc, which is based on high-keyed nationalist and racial issues, is going to give us much more difficulty this year than ever before.

As a consequence, the mood of the British, French and other Western European delegations is bitter. These delegations are determined to fight against attacks on their colonial policies, but it is a retreating, holding operation in which their prospects for success are small. If the Arab-Asian bloc pushes the GA too hard, the reaction of the Western European and Commonwealth states may be violent. In the case of South Africa, whose segregation policies are for the first time under direct attack, there is serious danger that the Delegation may actually withdraw from active participation in the Organization. If this should initiate a general trend on the part of the French and other colonial powers, the result may be the most serious internal threat the UN has yet had to face.

For a while, the French had their backs up over an affirmative vote by us that the Political Committee take up the Tunisia and Morocco items immediately following the debate on Korea. This vote was cast in a situation in which, according to our estimate, the outcome would have been the same however we voted. By so voting, we were able to pick up a little leverage with the Arab-Asian group which may enable us to moderate the debate when the items are discussed. We have talked to the French both here and in Paris, and while their reaction is still acute, I think their initial sharp reaction is subsiding. They are faced with such an unstable and inflamed political situation at home that they are having a very difficult time here, and are difficult for us to deal with as a consequence. However, they have joined with us in sponsoring the resolution on Korea, thus indicating that we do not have a serious division on our hands, at least so far.

The Political Committee began its work on the Korean item Thursday. During the first day of debate, we had a majority against issuing an invitation to the North Koreans but the voting indicated that many of our Asian friends were still inclined to sit on the fence. Therefore, in my opening statement yesterday, I felt it necessary to lay it on the line pretty heavily, to show who started this business, and to remind the members how earnestly we have tried to restore peace in Korea, without any cooperation from the Communists. Reactions afterward indicated that we picked up considerable support as a result of this approach. We have introduced a resolution which would vote confidence in the way the United States has conducted the negotiations in Korea, and explicitly in our position on prisoners of war; the resolution would also call on the Communists to agree to an armistice on a basis consistent with the principle of non-forceable repatriation. Twenty other governments have joined with us in sponsoring this resolution. This includes virtually all the governments with troops in Korea. I believe we stand a good chance of presenting a good firm majority on Korea, which may have an effect on the Communist expectations.

By putting heavy stress on the Soviet responsibility for the Korean affair in my presentation yesterday, I feel that we may have helped to increase the liability to the Russians of a continuation of the Korean episode, and particularly to make them feel the contradiction between this running sore in Asia and their pretensions of peace. I hope this speech will have met at least some of the requirements of the speech you spoke to David Bruce about having me do here.

I felt it necessary to dispel the impression Vishinsky was trying to create, that the Communists had really offered some new concession in their note to General Harrison of October 8th. So far, there has been no indication that the Russians are ready to make any genuine move on Korea, but we are watching the situation closely.

In summing up the situation here, it appears to me that our principal job is to hold our friends and allies together in the face of a determined Soviet effort to drive wedges between us. Although we are still in the very early stages of this session, I think it looks reasonably promising so far. By starting out with a tone of moderation and letting the Soviets hang themselves with their own invective, we have picked up support from some of our friends with neutralist tendencies.

I have been endeavoring to do as much in the way of informal contacts here as possible, particularly with Latin American and Middle Eastern representatives. This kind of personal spade-work is extremely useful, not only here, but in terms of our work on many other problems.

According to present indications, the Soviet reply to my statement in the Political Committee on Korea may come early next week. Because of the importance of the Korean issue, I believe I should remain here at least through the first rebuttal to Vishinsky's presentation, and then take a new reading on how much longer it would be useful for me to remain.

Most respectfully, Dean Acheson

The Menon Cabal

On October 28 Selwyn Lloyd, British Minister of State, who was substituting for Eden, told me of a plan Krishna Menon was hatching. Lloyd purported to regard it as dubious, though I soon discovered that he was deep in it too. The idea—Menon refused to reduce anything to writing—was to turn the prisoners over to a commission under vague instructions looking toward repatriation. Menon was said to argue that this would produce an armistice and any arguments about its administration would be between the Communists and the "protecting powers"—that is, the commission—

rather than with the United Nations Command. I strongly opposed this nebulous idea, which had every vice, since the Eighth Army would have to control the prisoners and bear all of the risks of a breakdown in the armistice without any control over the administration of the vital prisoner-release part of it. On October 31 a talk with Mike (Lester B.) Pearson revealed that he had joined the cabal too. I told him, as my minute recalls, "that his interest in these proposals bothered me a great deal and implored him to keep in very close touch with me." I noted to my assistants that "this is a dangerous situation which we should watch very closely."

A return to Maryland to vote made possible a talk with the President and a report that in view of General Eisenhower's imminent trip to Korea it was very doubtful whether the General Assembly would support our twenty-one nation resolution. It seemed impossible to get any expression of the General's views until he had made up his mind what, if any, liaison he would establish with us. The President told me of his efforts to establish one. For the present, we concluded, I should play a blocking, defensive game in New York. Also, he insisted, I should accept Prime Minister Louis Stephen St. Laurent's invitation to pay an official visit to Ottawa later in the month.

A week later, Schuman and Eden having arrived in New York, the kettle came to its first boil. Ernest Gross, Acting Ambassador to the United Nations, and I probed Menon, Lloyd, and Pearson to the point where it seemed to us that Menon's fuzziness of expression and unwillingness to furnish any written text had enmeshed the other two in an about-face. It was, I wrote the President, "as they say in strike settlement lingo, [giving] us the words and the other side the decision." The result of their proposal seemed to be that those prisoners who agreed would be repatriated, and those who did not would be held prisoners until they did agree. In this way the principles of repatriation and of the negation of force both appeared to be observed. An earlier Mexican proposal that UN countries should each take some of the nonrepatriable prisoners as temporary working visitors would have met the difficulty more responsibly.

Eden, when he arrived in New York, had not had the education I had in the sophistries of Menon, Lloyd, and Pearson and, while agreeing with me that the prisoners should not be coerced into repatriation, was persuaded by Lloyd that Menon's ideas were not inconsistent with this. As fast as I would explain, Lloyd would confuse. In my letter to the President, already mentioned, I said that while all I needed for the moment was sympathy, a firm instruction would soon be necessary, since a definite break might be impending. Menon was proceeding on the pragmatic maxim that if you can't lick 'em, join 'em, while, following General Grant, I was prepared to fight it out on our line. Vishinsky's speech on November 10 had given us the kind of help prayed for by the preacher pursued by the bear: if it did not help us, neither did it help the bear. The Soviet Government, he said, would "not budge" on the prisoner issue. The Canadians thought the speech was not as bad as it might have been; the Australians, that the Chinese wanted an armistice but the Soviets did not; most of the Latins, Burma, Thailand, and the Philippines, that it closed the door. I added that it "slammed the door" but would be helpful in dispelling illusions. However, those of Menon, the Canadians, and the British were proof against it.

A series of futile meetings followed with the three and with the group of twenty-one—in which we pleaded for action and the British for delay, while Menon fiddled. I asked for instructions and got them from the President: ". . . inform the Secretary that the United States Government will strongly oppose any resolution which does not clearly affirm and support the principle of nonforcible repatriation." We were now almost ready for a showdown, first with the conspirators, and then in the General Assembly.

As I saw the situation, it was that the armistice terms had been almost completed at Panmunjom. Only the prisoner exchange, airfields, and armistice supervisory commission articles remained to be agreed. I was fully persuaded that the Communists would not reach final agreement with our dying administration, especially since General Eisenhower, who was highly critical of our management of the war, was going to Korea to form his own views. The twenty-one-nation resolution was intended to get Assembly support for the terms submitted at Panmunjom on September 28 and rejected, thus leaving our position with strong international support for our successors in office when they took over on January 20, 1953. Menon's attempt was to transfer the writing of the armistice terms from Panmunjom and the United Nations Command to New York and the General Assembly under the leadership of India and the Arab-Asian bloc with British and Canadian support. We were determined to prevent this.

Not yet despairing of persuasion, I made one more attempt to win the British and Pearson. At my request Secretary Lovett and General Bradley came to New York on November 16 for a meeting with them. My purpose was to get away from talk about what would influence the Chinese Communists toward an armistice and to have those responsible for the Eighth Army state clearly the dangers in the field that Menon's loose plan for dealing with the prisoners would present. My colleagues did their best but the meeting was too large; the talk wandered and did not have the effect I had hoped for.

The next day, November 17, Menon circulated his resolution, which had the defects I have already mentioned. At a meeting of the twenty-one delegations I spoke against Menon's resolution but offered to amend ours to incorporate a repatriation commission, provided it had a neutral chairman with powers of effective executive action. Eden and Pearson argued for taking Menon's resolution as a basis and carried a majority with them. However, a small group was set up to draft a revision of the Menon proposal. The United States was a member and asked to prepare a draft to work from. Long experience had taught me the advantage that lies in preparing the paper for discussion: the burden of making changes is on dissenters.

Other action seemed necessary to protect the interests committed to me. I met with the American press to discuss with them —not for attribution to me—those parts of Menon's proposal that were quite unacceptable to us. All of this appeared in the press at once and at considerable length. One of my hopes, as I returned to Washington at the President's call to meet with him and General Eisenhower about matters requiring action before January 20, was that the General might make some helpful statement on Korea.

A serious situation was developing in New York, I said at the meeting in the Cabinet Room. The debate so far had brought general acceptance of the idea that force should not be used to repatriate prisoners when an armistice took effect. However, some neutral nations led by India and supported by Britain, Canada, France, and some others sought to circumvent this principle in the mistaken belief that to do so would produce an armistice. They proposed that the prisoners be turned over to a commission, which should repatriate those willing to return and hold the others captive. The only escape from captivity would be repatriation. Certain results would flow from this: we would be justly viewed as having repudiated our own principle; we would have to use force to turn over the prisoners to the commission or hold them for its disposition; and we would have a precarious armistice, which would deprive us of observation behind the enemy's line and ability to break up concentrations and supply lines and would carry the constant threat of riots in the rear of our army.

The situation in New York called for energetic action on our part. A showdown was coming; debate would begin the next day and voting by the end of the week or early the next week. The President and his Cabinet advisers were firm. I had explained to our European friends that division among us on this essential matter would bring grave disillusionment in the United States regarding collective security, which would not be confined to Korea but would extend to NATO and other arrangements of the same sort. In this crisis a statement by General Eisenhower supporting the view held by the Government would be of the greatest possible assistance. I had prepared a suggestion for consideration, which I handed to Senator Henry Cabot Lodge. The General made no commitment, but the next day Senator Alexander Wiley, senior Republican on the Senate Foreign Relations Committee and a member of our delegation in New York, announced the General's support for the principle of no forcible repatriation.

A Showdown Impends

Back in New York on November 19, Eden and I met three times, twice with Lloyd, and then—at my request—alone. At the last meeting I proposed that he take over the management of the amendment for both of us, provided he would accept two minimum conditions below which we would not go: first, a neutral chairman with executive powers (we would refuse to turn over prisoners resisting repatriation to a commission paralyzed by the requirement of unanimity); second, an alternative to repatriation other than indefinite imprisonment. There had to be an end to their detention, though where they would go would obviously have to be worked out later, probably by some United Nations agency. Eden refused to commit himself. This, I pointed out, could only mean that he had already decided, or wanted to be free to decide, to infringe these conditions in concessions to Menon. There was another explanation, he insisted; if he made an agreement with me, he must inform Menon of it, which would destroy his influence with him. To me it amounted to the fact that we were not acting together, but at arm's length.

The struggle with the British and Canadians went on in and out of the group of twenty-one, and took the form of a debate not only as to how far amendments should go but also whether the Menon resolution should be given priority and whether this should be done before or after amendment. Eden and Pearson feared that Menon might withdraw his resolution—which had become the accepted vehicle of action—if it was treated severely. At this point I was unwilling to trust anyone, an attitude in which I found an ally in Sir Percy Spender, who had been made chairman of the subcommittee of the twenty-one. Sir Percy had been left as chairman of the Australian delegation when Richard Casey went home, instructed, however, to support the Menon resolution, with which Spender did not agree. He decided to construe his instruction broadly, agreeing with me to try to get Menon amended before we supported him—what might be called a "cash and carry" proposition. The amendments were worked out; the British wanted to negotiate with Menon; Spender would put them to the subcommittee on Friday, November 21.

This was the day on which I was making an early-morning flight to Ottawa for my state visit. Pearson was supposed to go with me but at the last moment sent word that his duties as President of the Assembly precluded it. By separating, each left his rear exposed to hostile action, but I had an energetic and able lieutenant, Ambassador Ernest Gross, in charge in New York. The struggle in the subcommittee produced a draw; no action was taken.

Canadian Interlude and Finale

Prime Minister St. Laurent, a charming and courteous gentleman, gave us a warm welcome and a delightful visit in Ottawa. On Saturday morning he invited me to attend a meeting of the Canadian Cabinet, the first time, he said, that any member of another government not a member of the Commonwealth had done so. The Prime Minister made a graceful speech of introduction. Other members echoed his welcome. Many of them knew some of my mother's family and the older ones had known my father. Mr. St. Laurent suggested that my hosts would be interested in any reflections I might share with them out of a long and varied service in government. Not without some purpose, I spoke about the problems that the new mass diplomacy posed in conducting international discussion through assemblies and public debate. The model—legislative procedure in democratic countries—was very ill adapted to the wholly different facts of international meetings, as I had just been observing in New York. The basic anomaly that struck one was the vast separation that existed between the few with the responsibility and capability for taking whatever action might be necessary and the many not only willing but eager to prescribe what that action should be and how it should be managed. I gave as an illustration the prisoner-of-war issue in New York and the opinion of our military on the dangers of an armistice unaccompanied by a prompt and complete disposition of the prisoners, of whom tens of thousands would fight repatriation or indefinite captivity.

At this point my good friend Brooke Claxton, Minister of Defense, interjected that he and many people thought our generals were wrong about this. I replied that his report brought out my point. Our generals were on the spot and in command—at the request of the United Nations—of six American divisions and twelve Korean divisions, equipped, trained, and supported by us, who with welcome but token assistance from others were fighting this war. It seemed to me that the military opinion that should be listened to was that which bore the responsibility of command. The Prime Minister agreed; so far as he was concerned, he said, there was no answer to that observation. The point had been made where it counted, and no more talk seemed necessary. Our visit ended with a luncheon at Government House given by the Governor General and a dinner given by the American Ambassador, Stanley Woodward, for the Prime Minister. On Sunday morning we returned to New York with pleasant memories.

There high agitation reigned. Ernest Gross had reported to me in Ottawa the unproductive results of his talks with Eden and Pearson and theirs with Menon. We agreed that their position was unacceptable and that he should tell them we would oppose it in the First Committee and put forth our own amendments. This he did, and apparently enough of his fighting spirit carried through to a press conference so that *The New York Times* of November 23 carried a story of a major break between the British and ourselves. Gross was upset about this, as were the British, but it seemed to me time to shed some light on the intrigue. Everyone would think that his was a calculated indiscretion, so we might as well act as though it were. When Pearson called me on the telephone and later saw me, he seemed much more cooperative.

Before the group of twenty-one met that evening, Menon had circulated amendments that met some but not all of our objections. At the meeting I urged that we stop negotiating with Menon, adopt the additional amendments necessary, and report out the amended resolution. What was needed were clear provisions both for terminating the repatriation procedure at a definite time after the signature of the armistice and for some other disposition of those prisoners unwilling to accept repatriation. While Lloyd asked and was given another chance to move Menon, two events occurred the next day, the twenty-fourth, that resolved the crisis: the President authorized me to go forward with our own proposal despite the British, and Vishinsky publicly and harshly rejected Menon's initiative. Here was another illustration of the Russians uniting us after we had gotten ourselves thoroughly divided. It quite destroyed the impression, assiduously cultivated by Menon, that he was in touch with the Communist side and that they were in sympathy with his efforts.

I followed Vishinsky before the First Committee, expressing sorrow at his disruptive attitude toward agreement on an armistice and praising the statesmanship of Eden and Menon. A few minor amendments would bring the resolution in accord with the admirable purposes stated in their speeches. I urged that these be made. A week of some confusion followed, during which Eden went home and I wanted to. Upon learning that the Chinese had endorsed Vishinsky's views, Menon wanted to withdraw his resolution but was induced not to. The final form of the resolution began to crystallize. The Latin American states lined up with us. "Events in the past twenty-four hours," I telegraphed the President, "have moved swiftly here and with all the elements of an old-fashioned melodrama." On December 1, the First Committee amended the resolution to provide a workable commission and assure that three months after the armistice was signed the repatriation procedure would end. Provisions for remaining prisoners, if any, would be determined by either a political conference or the United Nations itself. The General Assembly on December 3 adopted the resolution by a vote of 54 to 5, and Mr. Pearson sent it to Peking with a conciliatory note.

Ten days later the Chinese flatly rejected it and the North Koreans followed suit. At the same time the Communist prisoners in our compounds at Pongam-do refused to obey orders to cease military drilling, hurling missiles at troops who tried to enforce the order. In the resulting battle eighty-five prisoners were killed. Gromyko introduced a resolution in the General Assembly to condemn the "mass murder" of prisoners of war. It was defeated by 45 to 5 with ten abstentions.

AFTERWORD

IT WAS NOT SURPRISING that the Chinese and North Koreans rejected the UN December 3 proposal for the disposition of prisoners of war, with General Eisenhower's views on the war yet to be known. During the election campaign of 1952 he had announced that if elected he would go to Korea to look into ways of ending the war. He arrived there on December 2. The Chinese rejection came ten days later. On his way home—from Guam to Honolulu aboard the cruiser *Helena* with his prospective foreign affairs and military advisers—he reviewed the Korean situation. Arriving at La Guardia Airport on December 14, he made the first of several military statements and warnings—of deeds "executed under circumstances of our own choosing," echoed by John Foster Dulles—which suggested a widening of the war in case of continued stalemate. On the Communist side, Stalin's death on March 5, 1953, suggested that new leaders might also bring new and less restricted policies.

The war, to be sure, did take on a new violence in April, but not an expansion of area or an introduction of new weapons. It may be that the Communists wished to test the new Administration's resolution on the prisoner-of-war issue, or to improve the line of contact in the event of an imminent armistice. In any event, one of the heaviest offensives of the war won back for the Chinese Pork Chop Hill and Old Baldy. During the last two months of the war we sustained a quarter of the one hundred forty-two thousand American casualties of the war. The Chinese losses amounted to one hundred eight thousand. General Maxwell Taylor traded territory for this exorbitant price, which hardly suggests a decision by the new Administration to expand the war in the event of Chinese continuance of it.

However this may be, a new factor appeared upon the scene causing all parties to look with new favor upon an armistice. On June 4 the Communists accepted our final prisoner proposals, and on June 8 the armistice agreement between the United Nations Command and the Communists was completed, except for the final demarcation line. The talks had been boycotted by the South Koreans since May 25. President Syngman Rhee was single-mindedly determined upon reunification of all Korea as a war aim—as determined as General MacArthur had been. With the line of demarcation the only issue dividing the belligerents, he decided to enter the scene in a way that would keep them divided. On June 18, 1953, according to General Clark, "All Hell broke loose," when South Korean guards started letting loose anti-Communist prisoners of war. The reaction of the South Koreans was jubilance, with Rhee's popularity rising to intoxicating heights; of the United States Government, anger with Rhee, shock, apprehension of war with Peking, and threats and concessions to bring Rhee in line again. On the Communist side, Rhee's action and hero status were bitterly resented and not to be endured. In heavy attacks (with nearly fourteen thousand South Korean casualties) the Chinese demonstrated their military power to smash Korean divisions almost at will, until American support turned the tide against the Communists. It was one thing for President Eisenhower to threaten the Chinese with deeds "executed under circumstances of our own choosing." It was quite another for President Rhee to do the choosing.

The next month, between mid-June and mid-July, was a sobering experience for all parties. On July 19, 1953, the Communist command signaled the United Nations command that it was ready for an armistice, and was reassured, in return, that the latter would not support unilateral action by the Koreans. This faced Rhee with certain destruction should he try to carry on the war despite an armistice agreement. However, he gained important concessions—a security pact with the United States, two hundred million dollars in economic aid, expansion of his army to twenty divisions, and commitments regarding the political conference to follow the armistice.

Fighting continued unabated until July 19, when delegates resumed negotiations at Panmunjom. An armistice was signed on July 27, 1953, and uneasy quiet spread over unhappy Korea.

INDEX

Air attacks on Manchuria, possibilities of, 73–74, 77, 78–79
Air attacks on North Korea, 94
  Great Britain and, 135–36; MacArthur's orders on, 64–68
Air Force, Fifth (U.S.), 64
Alexander, Harold R. L. G., 135
Allied Control Council (Berlin), 11
Allison, John, 53
Almond, Edward M., 69
Anderson, Orville C., 84
Anderson, Vernice, 60–62
Anglo-Indian peace initiatives, 35–39
Antung, 64–65
Appropriations for the Korean War, 40–41
Argentina, 52
Armistice, moves toward, 115–27
  decision to negotiate through Ridgway, 121–25
  foul-up of, 122–25
  Kennan-Malik talks, 119–21; negotiations at Panmunjom, 126–27; negotiations and resumption of fighting, 125–26; peace feeler, 119; See also United Nations
Army, U.S., in Korean War (Eighth Army and X Corps), 46, 56, 62, 70, 126
  China offensive and, 115–16; defense of Japan and, 96; MacArthur splits, 68–69, 76, 77; Ridgway takes command of, 92–93; 99–100
Army of South Korea, Seventh Regiment of Sixth Division of, 62–63
Atomic Energy Commission, United Nations, 9
Atomic weapons, 9, 13
  Attlee mission to Washington and, 84–91; possible use of in Korean War, 77
Attlee, Clement R., 35, 77
  mission to Washington of, 84–91
Austin, Warren R., 16, 45, 57, 78
Australia, 57
Austria, 1–2
Baillie, Hugh, 100–101
Bajpai, Sir Girja, 37–38, 39, 78
Barkley, Alben, 74
Baruch, Bernard, 9, 86
Battle, Lucius, 101, 107
Berlin, 1
  blockade of (1948), 11–13
Berlin, Congress of (1878), 86
Bevin, Ernest, 36–37, 69
Biffle, Leslie, 107
Blockade of Berlin (1948), 11–13
Bloody Ridge, 126
Bohlen, Charles E., 23, 119
Bombing of Manchuria, possibilities of, 73–74, 77, 78–79
Bombing of North Korea, 94
  Great Britain and, 135–36; MacArthur's orders on, 64–68

Bradley, Omar N., 16, 18, 20, 32–33, 74
  Anglo-Indian peace initiatives and, 35, 37; relief of MacArthur and, 104–105
Brannan, Charles F., 32
Brazil, 57
Brewster, Owen, 111
Bridges, Styles, 24, 106
British Foreign Office, 35, 52
Bruce, David K. E., 141
Brussels Defense Pact (1948), 11
Burke, Arleigh A., 121n
Byrnes, James F., 2, 6
Canada, 35, 52
  U.N. Korea negotiations and, 146–48
Canning, George, 5
Casey, Richard, 146
Casualty figures of the Korean War, 129
Causes of the Korean War, 3–14
  blockade of Berlin, 11–13; Soviet aggressive moves, 8–11
Central Intelligence Agency (CIA), 53
Chapman, John Jay, 84
Chiang Kai-shek, 3, 14, 28–29
  MacArthur's support of Formosa and, 42–46
China, see Communist China; Formosa
China Aid Act (1948), 3
Chongchon River, 63, 70
Chosan, 62
Chou En-lai, 54–55, 93
Chungjo-Yongwon-Hungnam line, 56
Church, John H., 28
Churchill, Sir Winston, 6, 84, 86, 135
Clark, Mark, 20, 116, 133, 150
  takes Far Eastern Command, 128–29
Claxton, Brooke, 147
Clay, Lucius D., 12
Cobb, Frank I., 87
Collins, J. Lawton, 21, 74, 94, 97–98
  as Chief of Staff of Army, 28; mission to Korea of, 77, 83; as possible replacement for MacArthur, 82
Colson, Charles F., 133
Comines, Philippe de, 87
Communist China, 36, 73–76
  clashes with MacArthur's troops, 62–63; offensive of, 115–16; threats to enter war of, 54–55; U.N. embargo of, 118–19; U.N. negotiations with, 93–94; Washington opinions of possible intervention of, 78–81
Connally, Tom, 22, 24, 91, 107, 122
Constitutionality of Truman's Korean War decisions, 32–34
Cory, Thomas, 119
Council of Economic Advisers, 40
Craigie, Laurence C., 121n
Crawford, Boyd, 107
Crossing the 38th parallel, 49–57
  debate about, 49–53; instructions to Mac-

Arthur on, 55–57, 58–59
Cuba, 57
Czechoslovakia, 11
Davis, Arthur C., 109
Dean, William F., 33
Dewey, Thomas E., 26
Dodd, Francis T., 133
Donaldson, Jesse M., 32
Douglas, Lewis, 36
Dulles, John Foster, 21–22, 29, 107, 149
Early, Stephen, 46
Eaton, Charles A., 24, 25, 122
Eden, Anthony, 134, 135–36
  mission to U.N. of, 142–48
Eighth Army (U.S.), 46, 56, 62, 70, 126
  Chinese offensive and, 115–16; defense of
  Japan and, 96; MacArthur splits, 68–69,
  76, 77; Ridgway takes command of, 92–
  93, 99–100
Eighth U.S. Cavalry, 63
Eisenhower, Dwight D., 149–50
Eliot, Charles W., 84
Embargo of China and North Korea, U.N.,
  118–19
England, 52
  Anglo-Indian peace initiatives, 35–39;
  bombing of Korea and, 135–36
Entezam, Nasrollah, 93
Evans, Barbara, 107
Ferguson, Homer, 103
Fifth Air Force (U.S.), 64
Fifth U.S. Cavalry, 63
Financing the Korean War, 40–41
First Marine Division, 46
Fisher, Adrian, 110
Foreign Assistance Act (1948), 11
Foreign Ministers' Conference (Paris, 1949),
  12, 13
Formosa (Taiwan, Nationalist China), 4,
  14, 20–21, 25, 37, 38
  MacArthur's support of, 42–46
France, 52
Francis I (King of France), 87
Franks, Sir Oliver, 85–86, 90–91
  Anglo-Indian peace initiatives and, 35,
  36–37
George, Walter F., 24
Germany, 1, 8, 9–13, 49
  blockade of Berlin, 11–13
"Glosters, The," 35
Grant, U. S., 72
Greece, 8
Gromyko, Andrei A., 35–36, 121
Gross, Ernest, 16, 57, 78, 119
  U.N. Korea negotiations and, 142, 146–
  47
Han River, 28
Harriman, W. Averell, 26–27, 32, 44–46, 60,
  80
  and relief of MacArthur, 104–105
Harrison, William K., 138
Hearings on relief of MacArthur, Senate,
  109–11
Heartbreak Ridge, 126
Henderson, Loy, 38–39
Henle, Ray, 76
Henry VIII (King of England), 87
Hickerson, John, 15–16, 18, 24, 51
Hodes, Henry I., 121n

Hodge, John R., 1
"Hot pursuit," 94
House, E. M., 87
Humelsine, Carlisle, 106
Inchon, 1
Inchon counteroffensive, 46–49
India, 52, 54–55, 133
  Anglo-Indian peace initiatives, 35–39
Indonesia, 133
"Inquiry into the Military Situation in the
    Far East and the Facts Surrounding
    the Relief of General of the Army
    Douglas MacArthur from his Assign-
    ments in that Area," 109–11
International News Service, 76
Iran, 1, 8
Isolationism, 4
Japan, 2
  defense of, 95–96; occupation of Korea
  by, 1; peace treaty with, 49; 38th parallel
  and, 124
Jenner, William E., 131
Jessup, Philip C., 15–16, 44, 60, 80
  Anglo-Indian peace initiatives and, 35;
  Blair House meetings and, 18, 24, 32
Johnson, Alexis, 101
Johnson, Louis, 49, 113
  Blair House meetings and, 20–21, 23–24,
  32; letter to MacArthur and, 45–46; as
  Secretary of Defense, 16, 55n
Joint Chiefs of Staff, 16
  instructions to MacArthur about crossing
  38th parallel, 55–57; proposals for Korea
  after World War II by, 1; relief of Mac-
  Arthur and, 104–105
Joy, C. Turner, 121n, 138
Kaesong, 56
  negotiations at, 122–26
Kansas line, 115, 123, 126, 128
Kee, John, 22, 24, 107
Kelly, Sir David, 35
Kennan, George F., 6–7, 23, 81–83
  memorandum on Korean situation of, 50,
  57; negotiations between Malik and, 119–
  21
Kerr, Robert, 107
Kimpo Airport, 16, 21
Kirk, Alan G., 35–36, 38, 120–21
Knowland, William F., 43, 91
Koje-do, 130, 132
Krishna Menon, Vengalil Krishnan, 38
  U.N.-Korean negotiations and, 141–48
Krock, Arthur, 76
League of Nations, 4
Libby, Ruthven E., 131
Lie, Trygve, 16, 45
Limited nature of Korean War, 34–35
Lincoln, Abraham, 33, 72
Lloyd, Selwyn, 135, 141, 147
Lodge, Henry Cabot, 145
London Daily Mail, 76
London Daily Telegraph, 103
Lovett, Robert A., 65
  Attlee visit and, 85–86; as Deputy Sec-
  retary and Secretary of Defense, 55n;
  House Armed Services Committee and,
  83; MacArthur breaking of moratorium
  and, 101–102; "posterity papers" of Mac-
  Arthur and, 80

Lucas, Scott W., 24, 32–33
MacArthur, Douglas, 1, 20–21, 28–29, 80
  breaks Truman's moratorium, 100–102
    Baillie interview, 100–101
    letter to Martin, 103
    March 23, 1951, statement, 101–102
  dangers of involving China in war of, 73–
  76; failure of northern attack of, 77–78;
  hard China policy of, 35; Inchon counteroffensive and, 46–49; instruction of for
  crossing 38th parallel, 55–57, 58–59;
  moves to the Yalu river of, 62–63; orders
  about bombing North Korea of, 64–68;
  plans to attain Yalu line of, 68–72; retreat to 38th parallel of, 87; support of
  Formosa by, 42–46
    Veterans of Foreign Wars speech, 44–
    46
  Truman's moratorium on government
  speeches and, 76–77, 101–102; Wake Island meeting with Truman and, 60–62;
  See also Relief of MacArthur; Stabiliza-
  tion of the Korean War
McCarran, Pat, 106
McCarthy, Joseph, 113–14
McCormack, John W., 24
McDermott, Michael J., 44
McFall, Jack, 22
Mainland China, see Communist China
Malik, Joseph, 18–19, 23, 25, 37, 39, 51, 88,
  93, 119
  negotiations between Kennan and, 119–21
Manchuria, 54, 56, 65
  hot pursuit into, 94; possibilities of bomb-
  ing, 73–74, 77, 78–79
Mansfield, Mike, 24
Marshall, Charles Burton, 119
Marshall, George C., 69, 72, 74, 78, 83, 121
  bombing of North Korea and, 65; Mac-
  Arthur's telegram and, 96–97; Marshall
  Plan, 10–11; possible Korea evacuation
  and, 80–81; relief of MacArthur and,
  104–105; as Secretary of Defense, 55;
  telegram to MacArthur of, 57
Martin, Hugh G., 103
Martin, Joseph W., Jr., 103, 104, 112
Marxism, 7–8
Masaryk, Jan, 11
Matthews, Francis P., 84
Matthews, H. Freeman, 23, 24, 44, 80, 119
Menon, Krishna, see Krishna Menon
Molotov, Vyacheslav, 2
Monroe Doctrine, 4–5
Moratorium on governmental speeches con-
  cerning foreign policy, Truman's, 76–
  77, 100–102
Morocco, 140
Morrison, Herbert, 125
Münster, 86
Muccio, John, 15–16, 54, 60, 80n, 99, 106,
  122
National Defense Production Act (1950),
  41
National Security Council, 13, 27, 53, 54,
  73
  NSC-68 (document), 40, 70
Negotiations, see Armistice, moves toward
Nehru, Jawaharlal, 38–39
Netherlands, 57

New York Times, The, 76, 119, 147
Nitze, Paul, 53, 80
North Atlantic Treaty (1949), 12
North Korea, see People's Republic of
  Korea
Norway, 57
Nuclear weapons, 9, 13
  Attlee mission to Washington and, 84–91;
  possibilities of use in Korea of, 77
Occupation of Korea after World War II,
  U.S., 1–3
Old Baldy, 135, 149
Operation Killer, 92–93
Operation Strangle, 135
Osnabrück, 86
Outbreak of Korean War, 15–31
  resolution of Security Council and, 16–19,
  25
Pace, Frank, Jr., 28–29, 106
Paik Sun Yup, 121n
Pakistan, 57, 133
Pandit, Mme. Vijaya Lakshmi, 37, 39
Panikkar, K. M., 54–55, 134
Panmunjom, negotiations at, 126–27
Patterson, Robert, 2
Peace feelers, 119
Peace initiatives, Anglo-Indian, 35–39
Peace talks, see Armistice, moves toward
Pearson, Lester B., 138
  U.N. mission of, 142, 144, 146–48
People's Republic of Korea (North Korea),
  51
  establishment of, 2; MacArthur's orders
  about bombing of, 64–68, 94; U.N. em-
  bargo of, 118–19
"Perilous Gamble or Exemplary Boldness?"
  (Rees), 119
Philippines, 21, 23, 52, 57
Pongam-do, 148
Pork Chop Hill, 149
Prisoners of War, crisis over, 128–36, 138–
  39
  revolt in the compounds of, 132–34; vol-
  untary repatriation of prisoners, 130–32
Punch Bowl, 116, 126
Pusan, 1, 33, 39, 46, 96
Pyongyang, 56
Pyongyang-Wonsan line, 72, 126
Radhakrishnan, Sarvepalli, 37–38
Rashin, 64
  bombing of, 49
Rau, Sir Benegal, 57, 78
Rayburn, Sam, 41
Rees, David, 47
Relief of MacArthur, 104–14
  communications mix-up about, 106–109;
  decisions about, 104–105; reflections on,
  111–14; Senate hearings on, 109–11
Repatriation of prisoners, 130–32
Republic of Korea (South Korea)
  establishment of, 2; Seventh regiment of
  Sixth Division of, 62–63
Resolutions on Korea of U.N. Security
  Council, 18–19, 25, 51–53, 57–59
  See also United Nations
Rhee, Syngman, 2, 22, 53, 91, 122–23, 125,
  150
Richards, James, 122
Ridgway, Matthew B., 58, 69, 81, 112

Chinese offensive and, 115–16; decision to negotiate through, 121–25; MacArthur and, 100–101; POW issue and, 132–33; as successor to MacArthur, 105; takes Command of the Eighth Army, 92–93, 98, 99–100; takes Eisenhower's command, 129–30
Roosevelt, Franklin D., 86
Roosevelt, Theodore, 33
Root, Elihu, 4
Rusk, Dean, 1, 29, 44, 65, 80, 101–102
    Blair House meetings and, 15–16, 18, 24, 32; Far Eastern Division of State Department and, 53; Marshall and, 82–83, 96–97; Wake Island mission and, 60
Russell, Richard, 109–11, 133
St. Laurent, Louis, 142, 146–48
Sariwon, 56
Schuman, Robert, 127, 142
Sebald, William J., 43
Second Corps, South Korean, 63
Semyenov, Vladimir, 119
Senate Appropriations Committee, 21, 22
Senate Armed Services Committee, 109
Senate Foreign Relations Committee, 109
Senate hearings, MacArthur's relief, 109–11
Seoul, 16
    recapturing of, 46, 92
Seventh Fleet, 21, 23, 25
Seventh Regiment of South Korean Sixth Division, 62–63
Sherman, Forrest P., 48, 83
Short, Dewey, 24, 31
Sinuiju, 64
Slim, Sir William J., 87, 89
Smith, H. Alexander, 24, 29–31, 32, 43, 118
Smith, Walter Bedell, 36
Snipers' Ridge, 135
Snyder, John W., 32, 95, 105
South Korea, see Republic of Korea
South Korean II Corps, 63
Soviet Foreign Office, 51
Soviet Union, 1–3
    aggression after World War II by, 8–13; attitudes of foreign policy of, 6–8; possibilities of Chinese support in Korean War of, 78–79
Spender, Sir Percy, 145
Stabilization of the Korean War, attempts at, 92–103
    final break with MacArthur, 101–103; on the Korean front, 92–93, 99–101; in Tokyo, 95–99; in United Nations, 93–94
Stalin, Joseph, 1, 6, 36
    death of, 149
Stratemeyer, George E., 64–65
Suiho Dam, 64, 135
Summit conferences, 86–87
Sweden, 133
Switzerland, 134
Taft, Robert A., 26, 94, 107
Taiwan (Formosa; Nationalist China), 4, 14, 20–21, 25, 37, 38
    MacArthur's support of, 42–46
Taylor, Maxwell, 149
Tedder, Arthur, 35, 37, 89
Thirty-eighth parallel
    debate about crossing, 49–53; establishment of, 1; instructions to MacArthur on

crossing of, 53–59; negotiations about, 123–25; retreat of MacArthur from, 87
Thomas, Elbert, 24
Thorp, Willard, 40
Three-Star Extra (news broadcast), 76
Tokyo press corps, 76
Triangle Hill, 135
Truman, Harry S., 1, 16
    blamed for MacArthur relief, 113–14; constitutionality of Korean War decision and, 32–34; moratorium on governmental speeches and, 76–77, 101–103; Wake Island meeting with MacArthur, 60–62
Truman Doctrine, 8
Tsarapkin, Semen K., 119
Tunisia, 140
Turkey, 8, 52
Tydings, Millard E., 24
United Press, 76
United Nations, 4
    armistice negotiations at, 137–48
        Canada and, 146–48
        Menon cabal, 141–46
    Atomic Energy Commission, 9; attempts to stabilize the Korean War and, 93–94; Communist China and, 36, 38; embargo of China and North Korea of, 118–19; establishment of Republic of Korea and, 2; Security Council, 16
        resolution on Korea of, 18–19, 25, 51–53, 57–59
U.S. News & World Report, 76
"Uniting for Peace" (Acheson speech before Security Council, 1950), 52–53
Unsan, 63
Uruguay, 52
Utah line, 115
Vandenberg, Hoyt S., 23, 74, 97–98
Van Fleet, James A., 106, 115, 116
Vienna, Congress of (1814), 86
Vinson, Carl, 24
Vishinsky, Andrei Y., 36, 38, 55, 143, 148
Voluntary repatriation of prisoners, 130–32
Wake Island meeting of Truman and MacArthur, 60–62
Walker, Walton, 46–47, 63, 68–69, 73
    death of, 92
Webb, James E., 18, 23, 44, 82
Westphalia, Peace of (1648), 86
Wherry, Kenneth, 29
White Horse Hill, 135
Whitney, Courtney, 113
Wiley, Alexander, 22, 24, 91, 110–11, 122, 145
Wilson, Woodrow, 33, 87
Wonsan, 56
Woodward, Stanley, 147
World War II, U.S. occupation of Korea after, 1–3
Wu Hsiu-chuan, 88, 93, 121
Wyoming line, 115
Yalu River, 56
    MacArthur moves to, 62–63; MacArthur plans to attain line at, 68–72
Younger, Kenneth G., 36, 37
Yoshida, Shigeru, 107
Yugoslavia, 8–9
Zafrulla Khan, Sir Muhammed, 139
Zorin, Valerian A., 37